HIDDEN
HISTORY
of
HELENA,
MONTANA

HIDDEN
HISTORY
of
HELENA,
MONTANA

Ellen Baumler and Jon Axline

THE
History
PRESS

Published by The History Press
Charleston, SC
www.historypress.com

Cover photo from MHS Photograph Archives, Helena, 954–177.

First published 2019

Manufactured in the United States

ISBN 9781467144018

Library of Congress Control Number: 2019950043

Dedicated to Rich Roeder, Dave Walter, Vivian Paladin and Harriett Meloy.

CONTENTS

Introduction: More from the Quarries of Last Chance Gulch   9

1. Getting Here from There: Helena and the Benton Road   13
2. Stopping Along the Way at the Sieben Ranch   20
3. What's in a Photograph?: Bridge Street, 1865   26
4. Life and Death on the Frenchwoman's Road   31
5. Before There Was Deadwood   35
6. An Oasis of Questionable Virtue: Seven Mile House   39
7. Helena's Public Heart   44
8. Red-Light Businesswomen   49
9. Trouble with Neighbors: The House of the Good Shepherd   55
10. Was Helena Invaded by Hairy Aliens in 1976?   61
11. The Hanging of the Golden Lanterns:
    Nighttime Airway Beacons Surround the Capital City   65
12. They Shall Not Pass: The Ground Observer Corps and
    the Helena Filter Center   71
13. Planting the Seeds of Saint Peter's Hospital   76
14. Unraveling the Myths of Helena's Chinatown   81
15. The Joe Louis of the Mat: The Saga of "King Kong" Clayton   87
16. To Ornament the City: Jewish Landmarks   92
17. Building a Better Helena: The Southside Lime Kilns   98
18. Haunting on Holter Street   104
19. The Great Canyon Ferry Flying Saucer Hoax   110
20. Bryant School's Unusual Friends   113

Bibliography   119
Index   123
About the Authors   127

More from the Quarries of Last Chance Gulch

For many, Helena's remarkable history consists of just a few items: the Four Georgians, the upper West Side's mansions, the 1935 earthquakes, the Marlow Theatre and Urban Renewal. It is much more than that. True, the above definitely impacted the city and our understanding of it, but ultimately, the Queen City's history is about people and events. Most of those people are largely forgotten. A few who had an effect on the development of the place, however, stand out. Events are also sometimes forgotten unless they were spectacular or had some lasting impact. This modest volume attempts to flesh out some of Helena's vibrant history from the inside. It tells the story of people who you have probably never heard of, events that have been largely forgotten and places that are taken for granted or no longer exist. We also hope to clear up some misconceptions, dispel a few myths and tell some little-known stories. We hope you enjoy them.

This book has its genesis in the spring of 1995, when seven Montana historians gathered in Rich Roeder's living room to discuss the idea of writing a weekly newspaper column on Helena's history. Among those gathered was longtime *Independent Record* editor Dave Shors, who supported our effort and provided encouragement. In addition to Roeder and Shors, the group included Dave Walter, Chere Jiusto, Harriett Meloy, Leanne Kurtz and the two authors of this volume. The discussion was animated, optimistic and sometimes raucous, as discussions among historians can sometimes be. The result was "More from the Quarries of Last Chance Gulch." We took the title from Will Campbell's monumental mid-twentieth-century work *From the Quarries of Last Chance Gulch*, an important two-volume compendium of Helena's news history and one of the most important sources for Helena's early history. Our weekly column ran in the *Independent Record* from 1995 through 1999.

Those were heady times as the only restriction was that the column had to deal with Helena and Lewis and Clark County history. With the blessing of *Independent Record* publisher Bruce Whittenberg, we wrote about what we were interested in, satisfying old questions we may have had and informing our readers about what a great place Helena is. Topics ranged from the Guardian of the Gulch, Mark Twain's visit to Helena and Helen Clarke, to Bertie Miller, a cross-dressing footpad. In 1996, magazine editor Vivian Paladin and historian Kim Morrison joined the group. We bounced ideas off each other, sought advice about how to tackle particularly tricky or sensitive issues and just generally enjoyed our collective company during regular meetings over lunch at the Windbag.

Thanks to the support of Bruce Whittenberg, the *Independent Record* published the first of three compilations of the Helena history column in 1995. Two more followed in 1996 and 1998. The collections did not include all the columns published in the newspaper. Some of the chapters in this book include our columns not published in the three collected volumes. The authors conceived this work in the spirit of the original "Quarries" series. Over the years, the number of contributors to "More from the Quarries of Last Chance Gulch" grew to include thirteen local historians. But organizing and fact-checking a weekly column like ours was no small feat. Like the gold rush itself, the momentum eventually played out and contributors went on to do other things. The *IR* published the last "Quarries" columns in December 1999.

But also like many gold strikes, there was always the hope that new riches would be discovered, and the column would someday continue. The authors spoke about it often, especially after some new tidbit of historical information was uncovered or a past event suddenly came to light. Helena still has plenty of history to tell. It surrounds us on the city's streets, in the mountains and in the old newspapers. These are all full of historical gold. Maybe this book will reinvigorate that rush and encourage others to uncover more lost and forgotten nuggets.

Four of the "Quarries" original authors have since crossed over to the other side: Rich Roeder, Dave Walter, Harriett Meloy and Vivian

Paladin. Each made invaluable contributions to the understanding of, and appreciation for, the community we love. They inspired us. It is because of their contributions that we, the authors, dedicate this book to those four historians and friends. We hope that they would approve.

I

Getting Here from There

Helena and the Benton Road

By Jon Axline

Transportation was a big deal for the Montana mining camps, and for Helena it was no different. During its mining camp phase, the Queen City was fortunate to be at the hub of several major arterials and a network of smaller feeder roads that led to other mining camps in the area. A good road was the lifeblood of any community, but this is especially so for a remote mining camp in the wilds of the northern Rocky Mountains. From Helena roads radiated to Butte, Virginia City, Deer Lodge, Confederate Gulch and the Gallatin Valley. Perhaps the most important of all the roads was Benton Road between Helena and the steamboat port of Fort Benton.

During the summer of 1805, William Clark noted an abundance of aboriginal trails north of the Helena Valley. The valley, even then, was a crossroads for Montana's first citizens as they followed the bison herds in their annual migrations. In 1853, the federal government commissioned an extensive survey of the northern Rocky Mountains and the Pacific Northwest for potential routes for a northern transcontinental railroad. Through much of the 1850s, exploring parties crisscrossed the region in search of a good route for the steel rails. The most prominent of these explorers was a recent West Point graduate and lieutenant in the U.S. Corps of Topographical Engineers, John Mullan.

A firm believer in the railroad as a symbol of civilization, he was committed to finding the best way across the mountains for the proposed line. But he also concluded that a good military wagon road should precede the railroad. To that end, he and his boss, Washington territorial governor Isaac Stevens, convinced Congress to fund the construction of a wagon road from Walla Walla, Washington, across the Rockies to Fort Benton—the world's innermost steamboat port. Mullan and 230 laborers and soldiers began the task of building the 624-mile wagon road in 1859. The road, which followed old Indian trails, skirted the Helena Valley in 1860. Mullan, clearly optimistic about the valley's potential, described the valley in 1865 as containing "several small and choice localities for farms….I look forward with much hope to see all these creeks settled and fine farms developed under the hand of the Rocky Mountain farmer." He completed the road on August 1, 1860. The first engineered and the first federally funded road in the Treasure State, Mullan Road became the core of the territory's road network and, later, the modern highway system in western Montana.

Gold strikes on Grasshopper Creek in the summer of 1862 brought the first large numbers of Euro-Americans to the remote northern Rockies. Mullan Road was an important thoroughfare for pilgrims and supplies destined for the mining camps. Members of the Fisk Expeditions in 1862 and 1863 followed a northern overland route to Fort Benton and then navigated the road south over Mullan Pass to the gold camps. The pass west of Helena was a busy place in the early 1860s, and Mullan Road ruts still scar the meadow on top of the Continental Divide. The discovery of gold placers on Last Chance Creek in July 1864, though, changed the character and, eventually, the name of the road.

The rich gold strike on Last Chance Gulch drew hundreds of miners, businessmen and others to the Helena Valley. By the end of the year, freighters had blazed a trail from Mullan Road to Helena. Benton Road, as it became known, provided a significant lifeline to the settlement, enabling the importation of supplies critical to the survival and prosperity of the mining camp. It also facilitated the shipment of gold and other minerals back to the United States. The 130-mile route was well marked and easy to follow with stage stations located about every ten to fifteen miles along its length.

The first Benton Road configuration branched off Mullan Road at the Austin junction and followed Birdseye Road, Country Club Avenue and Euclid Avenue into Helena. It was the primary arterial into Helena from Fort Benton from 1864 until 1868, when the freighters blazed a new alignment. For a time, Andrew Glass operated a small stage stop and saloon, near where the road crossed Seven Mile Creek. Today, a collection of outbuildings and the remains of a false-fronted commercial establishment still stand at the site.

Hugh Kirkendall's mule-drawn freight wagons were a common sight on Benton Road during the 1860s and 1870s. *From MHS Photograph Archives, Helena, Stereograph Collection.*

By 1868, heavy traffic on the road led to the establishment of a second branch road to Helena from Benton Road. From Silver City, it mostly followed today's Lincoln Road and curved into the valley from the Scratch Gravel Hills. Once in the valley, Benton Road followed two routes to the city: one along today's Green Meadow Drive to Euclid Avenue and the other along the general alignment of North Montana Avenue. This alignment came into Helena via Gold Avenue and North Last Chance Gulch. This route eventually superseded the original Benton Road alignment to Helena and was the primary arterial into the city until the completion of the Northern Pacific Railway in 1883. Because the new road lacked the steep grades of its predecessor, it was easier for the heavy freight wagons to negotiate.

In the late summer months, an observer on the edge of town would have seen the freighters coming this way long before they ever saw a wagon or heard a bullwhacker cursing at his charges. Like many well-traveled roads at the time, Benton Road was not limited to a single track. During the summer months, the dust on the heavily used route, combined with the shortage of grass for the horses, mules and oxen, would have

Above: Freighters had to wait their turn to deliver supplies in narrow Last Chance Gulch. *From MHS Photograph Archives, Helena, 954–200.*

Opposite: The 1868 Government Land Office map showing routes of both Benton Roads in the Helena Valley. *From Montana Department of Natural Resources and Conservation.*

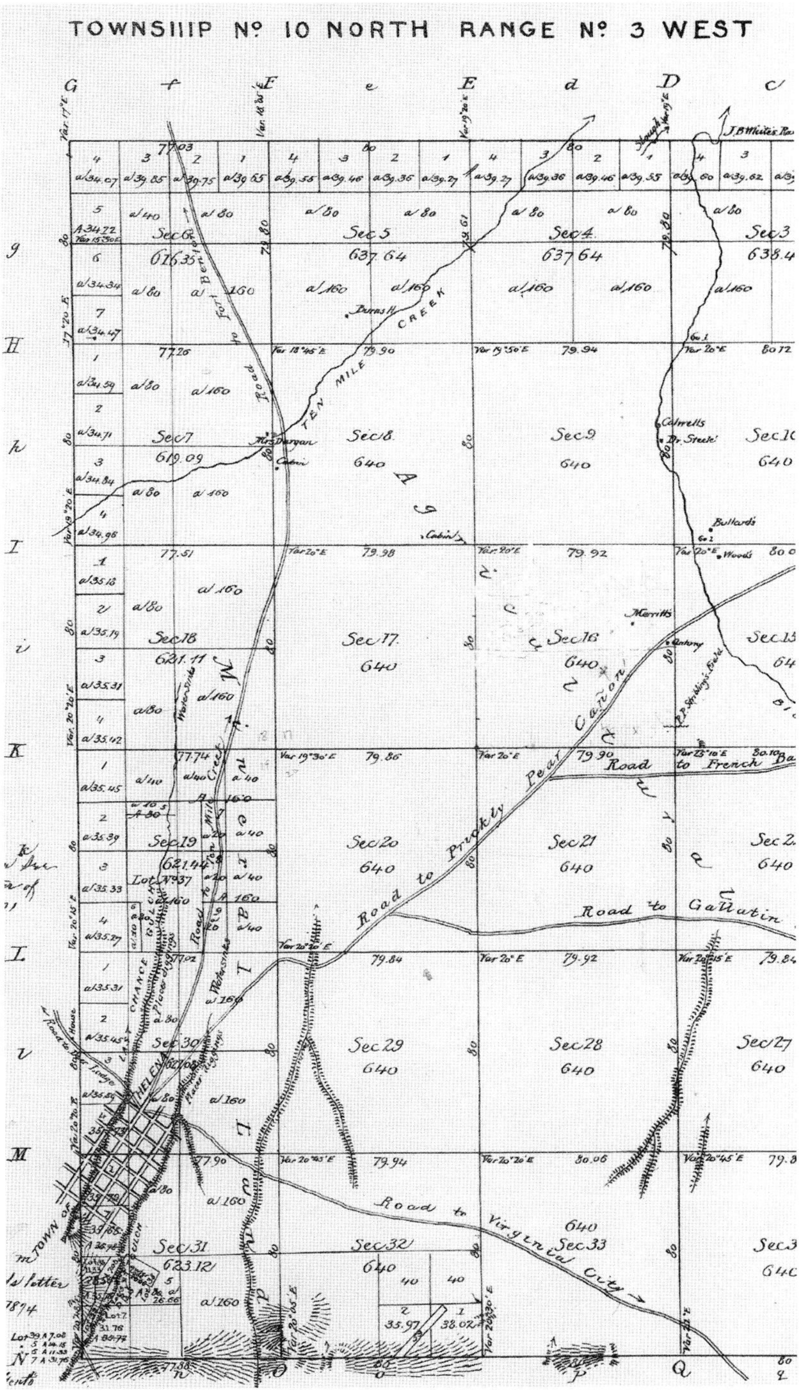
TOWNSHIP Nº 10 NORTH RANGE Nº 3 WEST
Sec 6
Sec 5
Sec 4
Sec 3
Sec 7
Sec 8
Sec 9
Sec 10
Sec 18
Sec 17
Sec 16
Sec 15
Sec 19
Sec 20
Sec 21
Sec 22
Sec 30
Sec 29
Sec 28
Sec 27
Sec 31
Sec 32
Sec 33
TEN MILE CREEK
Road to Fort Benton
Road to Prickly Pear Cañon
Road to French Bar
Road to Gallatin
Road to Virginia City
HELENA
TOWN OF
Mrs. Dargan
Cabin
Cotrells
Dr. Steele
Bullards
Woods
Merritts
Antony
CHANCE GULCH

caused the wagons to fan out. The road cut a wide swath across the Prickly Pear and Little Prickly Pear Valleys as it neared Helena. Ten Mile Creek got its name because it was ten miles from Silver City—the valley's first population center before the gold strike on Last Chance Gulch. Creek crossings provided mile markers of sorts for the freighters and coachmen who used the road.

Once the wagon trains reached Helena, they camped outside of town, either near the present location of the railroad depot or just off today's I-15 Cedar Street Interchange. Last Chance Gulch was too narrow to accommodate many wagons and choked traffic to Bridge Street, Helena's first commercial district. The freighters took turns driving their teams into the gulch and delivering supplies to the camp's merchants. A feeling for this Helena tradition can still be experienced by anyone who tries to navigate the gulch during the morning delivery times for the many businesses that line the street.

Although Helena folklore reports that Benton Avenue is the old Benton Road, there is no strong evidence that supports that belief. While minor portions of it may have been, historic maps of Helena suggest otherwise. Portions of Benton Avenue were originally known as Senior Street until March 1887, when the city commission designated it as part of Benton. The 1884 Sanborn Fire Insurance map of Helena indicates that Benton Avenue terminated at the intersection of Holter Street and later extended north past Carroll College to the combination city golf course and airfield. The street, moreover, was named in honor of the late Thomas Hart Benton, a Missouri senator and famous proponent of westward expansion.

Contrary to popular belief, the rock retaining walls adjacent to South Park Avenue were also not part of Benton Road. In fact, little is known about the road or the retaining walls. They do not appear in an 1875 Helena street map of the city but are apparent in an 1885 photograph of the Reeder's Alley area. The fire insurance maps show it as an "unimproved alley" but without the walls. It is not known who constructed them. The stone for the walls was likely quarried on Mount Helena by Jacob Adami and his sons. The old road, which is now closed to traffic, was certainly designed for wagon traffic, not for today's automobiles, and may have been part of the road to Unionville and Park City. The origin of the prominent retaining walls is one of Helena's enduring mysteries.

Sojourners today miss much of the adventure that travelers experienced on Benton Road in the late nineteenth century. No longer are they subject to broken axles, runaway horse teams, massive potholes, rickety bridges and price gouging by toll keepers. Indian attacks and the laboriously slow plodding of the ox teams are also a thing of the past. But motorists today still share the excitement and relief of rounding the Scratch Hills and seeing Helena spread out before them.

2

STOPPING ALONG THE WAY
AT THE SIEBEN RANCH

By Ellen Baumler

The Sieben Ranch in the Prickly Pear Valley is a special heritage place that reveals a diversity of human experience, a depth of contribution and an important pattern of stewardship. But its story, intertwined with the larger Prickly Pear Valley, began in the dim past when the valley lay in the shadow of the Bear's Tooth. This impressive landmark—two massive peaks resembling a bear's open jaw—guided generations of Native American travelers on the Old North Trail from Canada to Mexico. The MacHaffie quarry site near Montana City preserves evidence of these early migrations where the first people stopped to make tools some twelve thousand years ago. More recent Native American art on local cliff faces is further evidence of those who passed before.

Members of the Lewis and Clark expedition explored the region, naming Prickly Pear Valley for the painful cactus that penetrated their moccasins. They also knew about the Bear's Tooth from Nicholas King's 1803 map of the Northwest, which shows the landmark just above what the expedition named "Gate of the Rocky Mountains." Isaac Stevens passed through in 1853, scouting a route for the Northern Pacific, and John Mullan's wagon road eventually passed through the valley.

Malcolm Clarke was among the valley's first settlers. He left a tragic legacy. Twice expelled from West Point for fighting with fellow cadets, in 1841, Clarke signed on with the American Fur Company as a clerk at Fort McKenzie, above the later site of Fort Benton. Clarke's two wives—Coth-

The Bear's Tooth, sketched in 1868, guided travelers until an earthquake destroyed one of its tusks in 1878. *From A. E. Mathews,* Pencil Sketches of Montana.

co-co-na (Kohkokima), a Piegan woman, and Good Singing Sandoval, a mixed-race woman—made him an asset to the fur trade. But a fatal encounter with Owen McKenzie, son of Fort McKenzie's founder, forced Clarke to move his family to the Sun River experimental agricultural station, where he was hired to reverse its financial misfortune. This Clarke accomplished, but when Indian agent Gad Upson arrived for inspection, the carousing Clarke had fostered earned him prompt dismissal.

Clarke and his large family relocated to acreage in the Prickly Pear Valley in 1864, on the cusp of gold discoveries at Last Chance Gulch. The Clarkes offered primitive lodgings and fresh horses for the stage along the well-traveled Benton Road that skirted the Clarke ranch. Early Montanans esteemed Clarke for his thirty years in Montana. In February 1865, Clarke was among the twelve prominent Montanans who signed the act incorporating the Montana Historical Society. He had more longevity in Montana than any of them.

Acting territorial governor Thomas Francis Meagher and Judge Lyman Munson were Clarke's guests in 1865. They enjoyed champagne and a fine meal. Clarke's cultivated acreage, his prize horses and his accomplished daughter Helen greatly impressed Meagher. But saddles and blankets served as beds, and the men slept under a shed with their rifles loaded. While their picketed horses foraged around haystacks, sentinels patrolled the camp. Times were uncertain, and no one was entirely safe.

Good Singing died during childbirth in 1868, and in 1869, a dispute over horses prompted Coth-co-co-na's relatives to murder Clarke. He was buried in the nearby cemetery alongside Good Singing, their stillborn daughter Mary Ann and several of their other children. Retaliation for Clarke's murder led to the tragic Baker Massacre a few months later.

Malcolm Clarke was the first owner of the far-famed Sieben Ranch. *From Helen Fitzgerald Sanders,* A History of Montana.

Scotsman James Fergus and his wife, Pamelia, acquired the Clarke ranch and moved there in 1872. Fergus raised cattle; blooded horses; and marketed beef, grain, hay and potatoes. Pamelia ran the stage station, hotel and restaurant. She built a business, selling fifty to one hundred pounds of butter every week to restaurants, grocers and private customers. James Fergus was heavily involved in local politics, served on the Board of County Commissioners for most of the 1870s and was chairman from 1875 to 1877. Fergus also had a fine library.

After the Battle of the Big Hole in the fall of 1877, General William T. Sherman, commander-in-chief of the U.S. Army, traveled through Helena to visit recuperating survivors and stopped at the Fergus ranch. Upon inquiring about the small graveyard, he was shocked to discover that Malcolm Clarke, a fellow West Point classmate, was buried there. Sherman had regretted losing touch and always wondered what became of him.

The Ferguses weathered a personal crisis in 1876 when their youngest daughter, Lillie, got pregnant. Her suitor had left to buy land in Iowa. When he returned, Lillie was within weeks of delivery, and the time for a proper wedding had passed. The couple quietly said their vows, and James Fergus did not attend the ceremony. The newlyweds left immediately for their farm in Iowa. Despite Pamelia's efforts to keep the pregnancy quiet, all the neighbors gossiped about it.

Indians had warned early settlers about frequent earthquakes. Tremors and several quakes were recorded during the nineteenth century, including one that claimed the Bear's Tooth. In February 1878, a hunting party noticed a brief rumbling of the earth. When they reached the Bear's Tooth, they discovered one of its tusks—a perpendicular mass of rock three hundred feet in circumference and five hundred feet tall—had dislodged and tumbled down the mountainside, leveling an entire forest. The loss of the tooth left only one peak, and the landmark became a hazy memory. Its replacement, the Sleeping Giant, was not recognized until 1893. The giant's nose is the remaining tusk.

James Fergus intended to make substantial sums racing and breeding horses on his ranch. He paid an astounding $3,000 for two blooded stallions, Fayette Mambrino and Don A, hoping to realize substantial income from stud fees. Fayette Mambrino grew ill and died in 1878. It was an economic calamity for Fergus and many western Montana horse breeders who had counted on breeding their thoroughbred mares with the stallion. Fergus received dozens of sympathy letters. In digging the horse's grave on the

The Sieben Ranch lies in the shadow of the remaining tusk of the Bear's Tooth, known since the 1890s as the Sleeping Giant. *From author.*

ranch, workers uncovered the huge skeleton of a mastodon, once again recalling the valley's earliest history.

When the fledgling Montana Stockgrowers organized in 1879, James Fergus was among the distinguished men of the territory who signed its constitution. By this time, the township upon which his ranch lay was inside railroad limits. Ranchers could own no more than eighty acres—not enough to support his livestock. In 1880, Fergus sold the property to Martin Mitchell, and the Ferguses moved to the open plains of central Montana.

Martin Mitchell was one of the people who discovered the Gloster quartz mine on Silver Creek west of Helena. With profits from this mine, Mitchell purchased the Fergus ranch and hotel for $2,700. Soon after, he married Eliza Murphy, enlarged the house and offered travelers fine meals and comfortable lodgings.

By the 1880s, the valley supported many ranching families. Among them were the Hilgers, who brought the first tourism to western Montana, capitalizing on river excursions at Gates of the Mountains. The Montana Central Railway came through the Prickly Pear Valley in 1887. A station and post office, north of the ranch, were named for Mitchell. Portions of the hand-laid stonework reveal the difficulty of laying tracks through the canyon.

Eliza died of heart trouble in California, leaving three small children—one of them a newborn. Mitchell brought his wife's remains back to Helena for burial at the old Saint Mary's Cemetery. She still rests somewhere beneath the tended grass of what is now Robinson Park.

Once the railroad came through freeing land, Mitchell added acreage. He built a school at the ranch to serve local children, including future world champion bronc buster Fanny Sperry. Mitchell remarried in 1892 and served in the 1895 legislature. In 1897, he sold the ranch to Henry Sieben and Tom Grimes.

Henry Sieben was five in 1851 when his large family immigrated from Germany to Illinois. He and his brother Leonard journeyed west in 1864 and freighted goods along the Benton Road to Corinne, Utah. They often passed the Clarke ranch and probably stopped there many times. The brothers began ranching in 1870. Their brother Jacob joined them, and they added sheep to their cattle and horses. In 1879, Henry struck out on his own. He—along with James Fergus—was among the early members of the first stock growers' association. When he acquired the ranch from Martin Mitchell, it had grown to sixteen hundred acres. Tom Grimes headquartered there as manager, while the Siebens wintered in Helena. The log house Grimes built currently serves as the central residence.

Although Sieben was in the meat-producing business, he loved his animals and went to great lengths to care for his livestock, forbidding the use of whips. He even sent employees to market with the stock, making sure the animals were well cared for on the long journey. Today, the Lewis and Clark County portion of the Sieben Ranch Company—in its fifth generation of Sieben family ownership—stretches across thirty-six miles and produces Targhee sheep, a variety Sieben descendent Henry Hibbard pioneered.

In 2011, current ranch owners John and Nina Baucus discovered a cache of obsidian artifacts in a lambing pen on the ranch property. Montana Department of Natural Resources and Conservation (DNRC) archaeologist Patrick Rennie studied the recovered artifacts. Testing of the obsidian revealed that it came from Bear Gulch in Idaho some 450 years ago. This discovery brings the history full circle from the prehistoric travel corridor and hunting grounds to the modern ranching era. The ranch is now an ambassador of the stewardship of all its owners and a testament to the preservation of its many fascinating historic layers.

3
WHAT'S IN A PHOTOGRAPH?

Bridge Street, 1865

By *Jon Axline*

Historic photographs are gold mines of information, and a lot of Helena's history is shown in two photographs taken of Bridge Street by an unknown photographer in 1865. They show Bridge Street from its junction with Last Chance Gulch looking east toward the infamous hanging tree, the top of which appears in the background on the left side of the photograph opposite. It was Helena's first commercial avenue. Both photographs provide a wealth of visual information about early Helena, its architecture, transportation and the types of businesses that served the mining camp's residents.

When the so-called Four Georgians discovered gold in Last Chance Gulch in July 1864, it caused a minor stampede to the new diggings by opportunists in search of quick profits. By fall, only a few hundred men mined the gold and surrounding bars, while other men and a few women mined the miners by selling supplies and services to them. Because the narrow gulch was where the mining occurred, entrepreneurs sought adjacent areas to establish the businesses critical to the operation of the mines and the welfare of the miners. On Bridge Street a miner could buy supplies and find accommodations and professional services. Because of this, Bridge Street was an important early arterial and trade center in the camp. The street got its name from the wooden bridge that crossed Last Chance Creek at the foot of the thoroughfare.

False front buildings figure prominently in the photo. False fronts are inseparably linked to the American West and are, if nothing else, perhaps the most iconic of all architectural styles in the Old West. The style provided a sense of permanence and stability to impermanent mining camps. They made a street look more substantial than it really was. While the buildings are made of logs, the false fronts display sophisticated clapboard, shiplap and board-and-batten siding. Many have decorative pediments—some even made of tin. This is not too surprising since there was at least one tin shop on Bridge Street. All of the buildings appear to have glass windows. Since glass was not manufactured in the territory at the time, the glass either came up the Missouri River by steamboat or took the more laborious route north over Salt Lake City Road by wagon. Many of the roofs are sheathed in wood shingles. A few have porches and boardwalks. One building has pine boughs to provide protection from the elements and maybe a little shade for its customers. A false front facing east on Hill or Joliet Streets shows a façade constructed of lodgepoles and clapboard with a sawn wood frame.

Bridge Street in 1865. The top of the infamous hanging tree is visible in the upper left of the photo. *From MHS Photograph Archives, Helena, 954–177.*

The photographs show a wide variety of enterprises on Bridge Street. In 1868, businesses crowded the street from its intersection with Last Chance Gulch to the top of the hill. Prominent in the photo is Felix Poznainsky and Lewis Behm's Nevada Dry Goods and Clothing Store. Both men were European immigrants who came to Helena from Alder Gulch, where they operated stores in Virginia and Nevada cities. In addition to dry goods, the men sold "ladies dress goods," including silks, muslins and prints. The men dissolved their partnership in May 1868. Poznainsky continued to run the store, while Behm became a stagecoach driver. A man named Carpenter and W.C. Maurer also moved to Helena from Virginia City and opened a grocery that provided supplies, grub stakes and provisions for prospectors scouring the surrounding hills for the elusive mother lode. The business next door sold the perfect combination of pies, cakes, cheese and beer. Apparently, the owners were not very fastidious, as there is a pile of garbage lying in front of its porch.

Other signs along the street show a tin shop and a shoe store, as well as a storage and commission business run by Bond, Street and Charles Rea. Charles did double duty as one of Helena's first dentists. There were seven saloons, two tailors, a milliner and a lawyer's office. Harry R. Comly came to Montana Territory from Pennsylvania and set up his law practice in Helena in 1865. He was a prominent Helena attorney and politician until he left the city for San Diego in 1892. Waterman Baker and his brother, Egbert, ran a livery stable on Bridge Street until the 1870s. The stable is on the right side of the photograph a few doors down from Dr. Ira Maupin's Eagle Drug Store. Many of the merchants on Bridge Street were Jewish immigrants from eastern and central Europe. At least one, Moses Morris, enjoyed a successful mercantile career in the Queen City until his death in 1937. Five boardinghouses, including one run by Fannie Hendricks, provided accommodations for the camp's visitors.

Conrad Kohrs's Highland City Meat Market was one of five butcher shops on Bridge Street in the 1860s. A German immigrant, Kohrs came to Montana Territory in 1862 and quickly realized the real money was not in the backbreaking work of placer mining but in mining the miners. In this case, in providing beef to the miners who may have gotten tired of a steady diet of venison and beans. Kohrs was the father of the Montana cattle industry and went on to make a fortune raising stock and investing in real estate and hard rock mines. His Queen Anne–style mansion is one of the showcases on Helena's upper west side. As the name indicates, the business originated as a meat market in Highland City—one of several mining camps scattered along Alder Gulch 120 miles south of Helena.

Bridge Street offered a wide variety of goods and services to the mining camp, including Kohrs's Highland City Meat Market. *From MHS Photograph Archives, Helena, 954–179.*

Little knots of men and a few dogs stand here and there in the photograph. One can't help but wonder what the men are talking about, where they came from and what happened to them. The photograph also shows an assemblage of log cabins—some under construction—on the hillside on the right side of the photo. Many of the cabins provided quarters for the miners and businesspeople who worked on Bridge Street.

Five covered freight wagons climb up the street in the first photograph. The wagons were drawn by oxen, indicating the wagons were likely filled with non-perishable goods. Oxen were the mainstay of the freighting industry in Montana Territory before the arrival of the railroads. Oxen were generally reliable, relatively easy to manage and didn't require that feed be carried, as was the case for mules and horses. They were slow, though, averaging ten to fifteen miles per day. Bullwhackers drove the animals. They were experts not only in the use of the whip but also in the use of the most profane language imaginable. According to folklore, townspeople heard the bullwhackers swearing at their animals long before the wagons came into sight. Mothers covered their kids' ears and men no doubt appreciated the expertise of the vulgarities.

A typical freight wagon could carry up to four and a half tons of non-perishable goods, while faster wagons drawn by mules and horses usually carried perishables. The wagons in the photograph are relatively small compared to the enormous freight wagons that plied the road north from Utah. It is more likely that these were used by one of the many locally owned freighting companies that plied the roads between Helena and Fort Benton or Mullan Road from Deer Lodge and Missoula. The last wagon in the train appears to have only two yokes of oxen.

By the late 1870s, the number of respectable businesses on Bridge Street began to dwindle as their proprietors either relocated their stores and offices to Last Chance Gulch or moved on to more promising communities. Although the street retained a wide variety of businesses, as it had in the 1860s, its proximity to the red-light district on Wood Street (later Miller Street), one block to the north, undoubtedly impacted its reputation. By the mid-1960s, only run-down buildings and empty foundations marked what was once Helena's first commercial district. In the 1890s, the city fathers changed the name of the thoroughfare to its current name: State Street. Nearly all traces of the once-vibrant early commercial district have since disappeared. But as it was in the 1860s, the area remains a gathering place of sorts as Anchor Park.

4

LIFE AND DEATH ON THE FRENCHWOMAN'S ROAD

By Jon Axline

For a few years in the 1860s, Montana Territory was dependent on a network of toll roads and bridges. Beginning in 1865, the territorial legislature granted licenses to men who agreed to build and maintain roads, bridges and ferries. The licenses set the maximum amount a toll operator could charge travelers for the use of the facilities, as long as they maintained them in good working order. The system, while not particularly efficient, was a good way for the cash-strapped territory to develop a transportation system with no tax revenue. Some roads and bridges became part of Montana folklore and none more so than Frenchwoman's Road, west of Helena.

In December 1866, the territorial legislature gave Constant Guyot permission to construct and operate a toll road over the Continental Divide between the Little Blackfoot River east of today's Elliston and Ten Mile Creek, west of Helena. The eleven-mile road crossed the mountains at what would one day be known as MacDonald Pass. At eleven miles, the Frenchwoman's Road provided a shorter and more popular alternative to the torturous and often snowbound route over Mullan Pass.

Constant Guyot likely immigrated to the United States from Le Havre, France, in 1856. By late 1864, he had arrived at Alder Gulch and soon after purchased a ranch in the Ruby Valley. Like many would-be millionaires in 1860s Montana, he saw big money in operating a toll road. He sold the ranch and headed north to the Helena area. For more than a year in 1866

No photographs of the Frenchwoman have been found. A roadside historical marker on MacDonald Pass commemorates her contribution to Montana history. *From Ellen Baumler.*

and 1867, he carved a wagon road west of Helena. When completed in November 1867, his road became known for his common law wife, the "old Frenchwoman."

At the very beginning, Guyot relied on his wife to collect tolls and provide amenities to travelers on his road. Indeed, Madame Guyot was one of many female toll collectors in the territory. Although her association with the road lasted less than a year, it carried her name for years after her tragic death in 1868. While accounts of the Frenchwoman are glowing, reports about her husband are less than flattering—he was hard-drinking, argumentative and boorish.

The Frenchwoman maintained a hotel in a log cabin near Dog Creek at the junction of the toll road and Mullan Pass Road about a mile east of Elliston. Madame Guyot's hospitality was well known to the many travelers between Deer Lodge and Helena. The popularity of the route and her home cooking made her a very busy woman—and possibly a wealthy one. One room in the cabin served as a combination dining hall and sleeping quarters. While some men partook of one of her delicious meals, others in the same room were rolled up in blankets on the floor. While Madame Guyot collected tolls and cooked meals, her husband spent most of his time working a hay ranch about five miles away.

On September 3, 1868, a young boy herding loose stock ahead of the Cox family neared the Frenchwoman's cabin and, through the open door, saw her lying dead on the floor "weltering in her blood." Terrified, the boy raced back down the trail to tell his employer. Along the way he met Constant Guyot. Cox returned to the scene with Guyot and found the cabin ransacked, but the table was set for breakfast for two people. Madame Guyot was killed by a single gunshot to the head. The clock on the mantle had stopped at 8:25 a.m., shortly after Constant said he left the cabin for his hay fields. Investigators believed the murder had been committed by two people. The Frenchwoman had a good business collecting tolls and feeding passersby. Rumors circulated that she'd hidden anywhere from $400 to $7,000 in gold dust in the cabin. It was not known if the murderers found the hidden gold.

Authorities briefly detained two Beartown miners, Bob Fender and Steve Schultz, for the killing, but they were released after close questioning by Judge John Bill. While some details are exact, others are vague. A reporter for the *Montana Post* postulated that the Frenchwoman had been beaten and then shot in the face at pointblank range. The newly widowed husband put up a $1,000 reward, while Deer Lodge County added $500 to that amount, and Helena shopkeeper William Newland added another $500 to the pot. The *Montana Post*, true to its vigilante heritage, wrote the day after the murder that "if those guilty of committing the crime are discovered, we hope no legal technicalities, no rush wall jails may stand between them and the rope, for hanging is too good for them."

No one was ever brought to justice for the murder of Madame Guyot. Some people, though, suspected her husband committed the heinous crime. The couple was notorious for their domestic squabbles, especially when Constant was in his cups. He could not account for his time between when he said he left the cabin and when the crime was committed. The table set for two, some believed, was for Constant and his accomplice—a man named Ruelle. Perhaps because of the suspicions and his fear of the noose, Constant left Montana Territory soon after his wife's death. The Frenchwoman, however, left her mark on Montana history with her death as one of the state's first murder mysteries.

Perhaps the real mystery is the Frenchwoman herself. For someone whose cooking and hospitality was famous throughout the territory, virtually nothing is known about her, including her first name. Her appearance has been described as a "neat looking critter—black-haired, black-eyed, and sharp, and cute lookin'." Even her age is a guess. She may have been around thirty, but the tag *old* suggests she was much older. We do know she was a good cook and liked to talk, but her English was not good. A *Montana Post* correspondent described her shortly before her death as a "garrulous, gossiping, good natured dispenser of ranch eggs and trout and tortured English." She may have had a "highly accomplished" daughter in Paris, but it's a rumor that is impossible to verify.

In 1877, a Butte physician had a terrifying experience at the old Frenchwoman's place. After a hard day on the road, C.S. Whitford and John Vial stopped at the Frenchwoman's cabin for a meal and a place to sleep. By then, Elijah Dunphy had expanded the cabin so that it contained sleeping rooms separate from the dining room. Shortly after going to bed, Whiteford suddenly awoke, "staring at the hazy and dimly-outlined figure and form of a woman slowly advancing with outstretched arms toward the bed." After waking his companion, who saw nothing, Whitford was unable to sleep. Ninety minutes later, the apparition reappeared in the same corner of the room.

After two visitations, fatigue proved stronger than his fear. He dozed off. The spirit appeared one more time after the sun rose in the morning. Whitford's description of the apparition closely matches the few physical descriptions of Madame Guyot. He described her "ravenous black hair hanging in loose tresses down the back; face snowy white, narrow and pinched, with an indescribable expression of pain and sorrow." After placing her hand on Whiteford's head, the shade slowly faded away but not before "appearing as though she would speak and disclose some secret."

Today, motorists speed by the site of the Frenchwoman's cabin without realizing the history of the area or the tragedy that occurred there in 1868. Although the cabin has disappeared, Madame Guyot still rests somewhere in an unmarked grave near the site.

5

BEFORE THERE WAS DEADWOOD

By Ellen Baumler

The HBO series *Deadwood* immortalized Seth Bullock as the first sheriff of Deadwood, South Dakota. Founded in 1875, Deadwood was a rip-roaring mining camp when Bullock entered the scene in 1876. He served as Deadwood's first sheriff and ran a successful hardware business with his partner, Sol Star. He served as captain of Troop A in Theodore Roosevelt's famous Rough Riders during the Spanish American War, and President Roosevelt later appointed him U.S. Marshal. Before he launched his long and famous career in South Dakota, Bullock made a name for himself in Helena and in Montana.

Seth Bullock was born in Amherstburg, Ontario, Canada, in 1849 to George and Anna Findley Bullock. In 1860, rival politicians accused his father—longtime treasurer of Essex County—of embezzlement. Seth's mother was reputedly on her deathbed as his father was convicted and served a short jail term. George Bullock eventually won a new trial and was acquitted. After these events, the family history is murky. Seth left home as a youngster, and by the 1870s, he was in business in Helena as an auctioneer. He also served as Helena's fire chief. Bullock, a Republican, represented Lewis and Clark County in the 1871–72 legislative session, where he helped establish Yellowstone Park. He was elected sheriff of Lewis and Clark County in 1873 and served a two-year term from 1874 to 1875. During his tenure as sheriff in 1875, Bullock replaced the first log jail with a larger, more secure brick facility, dubbed the Bullock Hotel.

He also presided over the first legal hanging in the Territory of Montana.

The HBO series and various histories claim that as sheriff, Bullock hung a horse thief named Clel Watson and held off a mob in a legendary event. The hanging supposedly occurred on a built scaffold in front of a crowd. If this were the case, there would be ample documentation. However, there is no mention of this event in the press or elsewhere. Further, the name Clel Watson does not appear in any contemporary context. The facts leading up to the first legal hanging in the Territory of Montana are much more interesting than this fictionalized episode.

Seth Bullock of Deadwood, South Dakota—shown here in 1893—presided over the first legal hanging in Montana Territory in 1875. *From Dickinson State University.*

The case involved the shocking murder of Austrian immigrant Franz Warl, who was a thrifty, but prosperous, burner of charcoal. He was a good man—well liked and well known—and a longtime resident of Helena. His customers included Helena blacksmiths and other businesses that needed coal to fire steam engines and furnaces. Neighbors discovered his mutilated corpse near his charcoal pit between Colorado Gulch and Ten Mile. He had been gagged with a barber's apron. His hands were tied behind him with harness leather, his skull was crushed, and his neck was dislocated. The cord was still wrapped around his neck. Warl's large, ferocious dog had stood watch over the body but chewed away half his master's face and an eye, adding to the horror of the murder scene. Warl was known to carry substantial currency and gold dust. When authorities searched his property, they found more than $1,000 hidden under some old clothing in his cabin.

The barber's apron helped identify Frederick Shaffer—who ran a local barber shop—as one of the murderers. It did not take long for authorities to identify and arrest William Sterres (Stears) and William Wheatley as his accomplices, but Frederick Shaffer gave authorities the slip. First Sterres, then Wheatley, stood trial in Lewis and Clark County before Chief Justice Decius Wade. J.K. Toole was the chief prosecutor. Shaffer, the mastermind behind the crime, was captured in Bismarck, North Dakota. Authorities held him, anticipating the payment of a reward. When no reward was forthcoming, Shaffer either escaped or authorities released him. He was never heard from again.

The court learned that Sterres had a wife and two children in Minneapolis, Minnesota, and another wife and a child in Sioux City, Iowa. Sterres testified during his trial that he was in the process of buying Shaffer's barber shop. He had already bought some of Shaffer's equipment and sent it up to Fort Benton. He feared that if he did not go along with Shaffer, he would lose his investment and the opportunity to open his own business. Further, he claimed that Shaffer believed Warl had some $14,000 on his property. The three hoped to make Warl tell where he hid his wealth. But Warl wouldn't talk.

Sterres was convicted and sentenced to hang. Wheatley's trial followed with a similar verdict. Executions, according to U.S. tradition, usually took place on Fridays. In this case, the two hangings were set for Friday, August 13, 1875. At Sterres's sentencing, however, the crime for which he was convicted was not clearly stated. Due to this legal technicality, Judge Wade granted Sterres a new trial. It was the general belief that the judge allowed a second trial because he was hoping to gain new information that would help in pursuing Fred Shaffer. Wheatley was therefore the first to be legally executed in the Territory of Montana. The execution was not without difficulties.

From territorial days until 1983, Montana law specified that executions must be carried out near the jail in the county where the crime was committed. Sheriff Bullock had a scaffold built in the yard of the new Lewis and Clark County Jail, roughly where the current Myrna Loy Center (which replaced the brick jail in 1890) sits today. The law also required the presence of the sheriff, a physician, the county attorney and at least "twelve reputable citizens." Sheriff Bullock sent invitations as the law prescribed. The law also clearly stated that women, children and the public were prohibited from witnessing hangings, so the sheriff had a fence built around the scaffold.

Thirteen symbolic steps leading up to the scaffold's platform made the gallows so tall that the fence could not entirely shield it from public view. Sheriff Bullock realized that he could not prevent public viewing because several buildings crowded around courthouse square, and he knew that hundreds of people would climb the roofs. Privacy was impossible to enforce. So, Bullock moved up the hour specified in the death warrant from midday to just past midnight.

As Sheriff Bullock had anticipated, a thousand spectators crowded the rooftops to witness the hanging by the light of the moon. After the sheriff read the death warrant, Wheatley calmly walked from the jail to the gallows, deliberately climbed the thirteen steps and addressed the crowd. He neither

The county jail, no. 5 in this 1875 birdseye map, shows the fence and simplified representation of the gallows. *From Library of Congress.*

admitted nor denied his guilt, but he thanked his counsel, spoke of the pain of separation from his family in Iowa and asked forgiveness for all of his transgressions. The noose was carefully positioned around his neck, a black hood was placed over his head and his arms were bound to his sides. Sheriff Bullock cut the rope, releasing the trap, and Wheatley dropped. Doctors pronounced him dead after ten and a half minutes.

After a brief trial and a ten-minute jury deliberation, Sterres was again found guilty of murdering Franz Warl. Sheriff Bullock presided over Montana's second legal hanging at noon on October 28, 1875. Hundreds of spectators crowded the roofs and witnessed the execution.

Seth Bullock soon moved on to Deadwood, leaving the grisly business of hangings in Montana behind. For another forty years, hopeful treasure hunters listened to the stories and combed Franz Warl's charcoal pits, looking for the $14,000 treasure the murderers never found. Perhaps it still lies somewhere between Colorado Gulch and Ten Mile, waiting to be discovered.

6

An Oasis of Questionable Virtue

Seven Mile House

By Jon Axline

Rest stops along the road are an important part of the American driving experience. Instead of highway rest areas, gas stations and convenience stores, our ancestors in Montana relied on stagecoach stations to take a break, stretch their legs, use the outhouse and maybe get something to eat. The iconic stage stations so often portrayed in Hollywood westerns were located every ten to twelve miles along Benton Road. At the stations, hostlers changed the horse teams and passengers could get out of the cramped Concord stagecoaches or "mud" wagons for a few minutes. In some cases, the stations also provided accommodations for tired or stranded travelers or for those prevented from reaching their destination because of adverse weather. The station keepers were often under contract with the stage companies and cut corners with services to turn a profit. Whether the food was good at the stations was open to debate.

Some stops, however, were the product of private entrepreneurs who saw opportunity in the road and were not affiliated with the stage companies. In many cases, small ranching, farming and mining communities grew up around those havens. One of those places was just a few miles outside Helena on Benton Road. It is still visible to travelers today but is no longer the oasis it was more than a century ago. Seven Mile House stood where Benton Road crossed Seven Mile Creek. For a short time in the late nineteenth century, it provided accommodations for weary travelers and a place to quench your thirst. It was a stage stop, community meeting place, post office

This false front building is likely Seven Mile House. It was the center of activity on Benton Road beginning in the 1870s. *From author.*

and, occasionally, a place of dubious reputation. Many of the buildings associated with Seven Mile House still stand.

When exactly Seven Mile House began is unknown. It was established by Caleb Sears, a miner and rancher. "Captain" Sears filed a mining claim on Seven Mile Creek in the mid-1870s. By 1879, Sears had expanded his operations to include interests in hard rock mines in the Silver City and Marysville areas. He also raised horses and cattle. Sears built a hotel for weary travelers on Benton Road sometime during his tenure in the area. In June 1879, he sold his ranch/hotel at auction. In addition to the hotel, cattle and horses, he sold forty acres of pastureland, furniture, horses, wagons and harnesses. The successful bidder was Charlie Colbert, businessman Anton Holter's half-brother. Colbert came to Helena in 1876 and operated a saloon and billiard hall on Rodney Street before moving to Seven Mile.

Colbert and his wife, Bertha, ran a popular and profitable enterprise. The *Daily Independent* stated that Colbert, "with his usual taste, has fitted up the house and grounds in a tasteful manner," and Seven Mile House "was one of the best places to stop outside of Helena." His establishment was particularly well known for his wide selection of quality liquors. In September 1881, the *Independent* reported that a committee of Helena city councilmen and members of the Board of Trade embarked on Benton Road to intercept the Marquis of Lorne at Silver City. The intent was for the men to escort the nobleman and his entourage to Helena, where they would be feted by the city's glitterati. Unfortunately, the welcoming committee only got as far as Seven Mile House, where they stopped for a drink. One drink lead to many drinks, and by the time the now-tipsy group reached Silver City, the Marquis had long-since arrived in Helena on the alternate Benton Road route through the Helena Valley. The newspaper lamented that the "Marquis came to Helena as any other private citizen, without a flourish of trumpets or other distinguishing tokens of public honor."

After a down-and-out miner named John Burke shot himself in the head in Colbert's barroom in March 1882, Colbert leased the operation to Charles Baker and Nick Baatz. He sold his interest in the business to Baker in 1884. In May 1885, *Chicago Tribune* reporter John McCafferty wrote a travelogue of his trip to Fort Benton from the Queen City. In an article that appeared in the *Helena Weekly Herald*, the correspondent wrote: "Reaching the Seven Mile House in fifty minutes [from Helena], the horses were watered, while the other animals exhilarated in the sunshine of the interesting landlady. It is the headquarters of good horse range and necessarily proves an agreeable halting place." No doubt the "other animals" were McCafferty's fellow passengers who had a deep appreciation of Baker's young wife, Anna.

Not all owners of Seven Mile House were of the same sterling character as Colbert and Baker, though. In 1886, Baker sold the operation to W.J. Curran, a man of somewhat dubious reputation. He changed the name of the station to Sunnyside House. Despite that, everybody called it by its old name. He sponsored a St. Patrick's Day celebration and free community dances on a regular basis. But trouble followed and Curran became the center of attention in a disagreement with one of the territory's Chinese residents.

In May 1886, a Chinese man named Lee Sing stopped by the establishment, either on his way to Marysville or headed back to Helena. He had been employed as a cook at a Helena hotel and was carrying ninety-five dollars in his purse. Curran thought he saw an easy mark and coerced the man into playing poker with him at a dollar a hand. Sing won the first three hands, and Curran accused him of cheating. Sing denied it and tried to leave. The saloonkeeper then pulled out a revolver and proceeded to pistol whip the man and shot at him, robbing Sing of the ninety-five dollars he had saved. Former Silver City hotelkeeper Andrew Glass separated the two men, and Sing managed to get outside, where he waved a revolver and shouted obscenities at Curran. He went to the window and took another potshot at Sing.

Stagecoaches often stopped at Seven Mile House so that weary passengers could take a break from the road for a few minutes. *From MHS Photograph Archives, Helena.*

Even though both the *Daily Independent* and *Weekly Herald* printed all kinds of derogatory descriptions of Lee Sing, the newspapers were surprisingly supportive of him. By the time Curran acquired Seven Mile House, he already had a bad reputation in Helena. The *Independent* described Curran as a cattle rustler "not unknown to fame as the man who borrowed a green plow, then painted it red and claimed it as his own." In the wake of the incident, Sheriff Dave Churchill arrested Curran and threw him in jail. Judge Armitage set a $500 bond for the man, but he couldn't pay the money. Curran spent the next six months in jail until the grand jury rendered a decision about the incident. For an unknown reason, the grand jury dropped the charges and released Curran from custody. He sold Seven Mile House to Andrew Glass and left the area.

A native of Sweden, Andrew Glass enlisted in the U.S. Army in 1866 and served at Fort Shaw until his discharge in the early 1870s. His wife, Johannah, worked as a laundress at the military post. Glass may have participated in the Baker Massacre on the Marias River in January 1870. Johannah had a young daughter named Fannie from a previous marriage. After his discharge, the family spent some time at Sun River before moving to the Seven Mile area. In addition to running Seven Mile House, Glass also operated an adjacent store that provided dry goods and mining supplies to prospectors. Glass and a partner, Pete Wilson, worked a placer mine on Seven Mile Creek.

As it turned out, Glass was also not one of the community's guiding lights. In 1889, he and his stepdaughter attempted to extort money from Pete Wilson. Andrew and Fannie accused Wilson of seducing her daughter, Anna, and demanded he turn over his interest in the claim along with $500 cash and a horse and buggy. Glass threatened to have two of his Silver City buddies hang Wilson unless he complied with their demand. Wilson sued Glass in district court and won his case. The testimony revealed that Andrew's family was dysfunctional.

Two years later, in 1891, Johannah sued Andrew for divorce on the grounds that he had lavished his affections on another woman two years previously. When the judge asked why she waited to file for divorce, Johannah claimed that her husband had threatened her life if she took him to court. The judge granted her the divorce and compelled Andrew to pay $800 alimony. He sold a portion of his property and stopped paying property taxes on the rest of it. Andrew Glass then left Montana. His ex-wife stayed in Helena and died here in 1911.

It is not known when Seven Mile House finally closed its doors. It last appears in Helena newspapers in 1892 when Glass lost it because of his failure to pay property taxes. By then, Benton Road had largely been eclipsed by the Northern Pacific and Montana Central railroads, both of which passed very close to the property. Seven Mile House was an important part of Benton Road—a landmark for weary travelers before they entered the Helena Valley and an oasis for parched throats. It was, in essence, a late-nineteenth-century highway rest area.

7

HELENA'S PUBLIC HEART

By Ellen Baumler

The heart of any community is the place where its pulse beats, where people gather, where everyone is welcome. For a century and a half, the Lewis and Clark Public Library has continuously filled that niche. It was not Montana's first library. The first, depending on the definition, was at Fort MacKenzie in 1833. Major John Owen had a fine private library at Fort Owen by 1864. Virginia City founded a public library of sorts in 1865. Although Virginia City's library was accessible to the public, it lapsed early on and was not reorganized until 1902. Helena's claim of the first *continuous* public library is valid.

The Helena Library Association formed in 1868. Its four founding pillars were attorneys Wilbur Fisk Sanders and Cornelius Hedges, hotelier Ben Stickney Jr. and miner James Whitlatch. Many attended the first formative meeting in late 1868. At the group's request, these four men formed a committee to solicit donations to procure a library, and they became instrumental in achieving this goal.

By the end of 1868, the subscription library—charging an annual membership fee—had established quarters on the first floor of the Whitlatch Building at the northeast corner of Jackson and Broadway. At about this same time, the *Montana Post* moved its plant from Virginia City to Helena and settled in the Whitlatch Building as well. *Post* publisher Ben Dittes was appointed as the first librarian. Association members went door to door with wheelbarrows, collecting donated books.

The library association soon announced a series of six lectures held at the Methodist Episcopal Church to raise funds for the library. At a dollar admission per lecture, or five dollars for the series, the *Montana Post* promised "the paltry pittance of admission fades into insignificance" when compared to the great benefits of the educational material and the worthy cause it would help fund. In March, the *Post* pronounced the series a rousing success; throughout the series, Helena's most prominent citizens had filled the spacious lecture room. Donations and subscriptions, including donations of publications from the Smithsonian Institute, soon amounted to $4,000.

Ben Dittes sold the *Post* in 1869, and the library moved its twenty-five hundred books to the Holter and Hedges Building, a two-story brick structure on South Main Street (now Last Chance Gulch). Wilbur Sanders had a suite of rooms on the second floor where he kept his office and his law library. Additional rooms housed the Helena Library Association and the Montana Historical Society's collections. The building was coincidentally located roughly at the northeast corner of the present Lewis and Clark Library.

Helena's early history is intertwined with spectacular fires that took great chunks of the community. One of those fires, in August 1872, began on lower Broadway and worked its way up to Courthouse Square. The Whitlatch Building was one major loss, along with the *Rocky Mountain Gazette* and several fine residences. Fortunately, the library had long vacated its first home.

The library was not so lucky a few years later. In the early morning hours of January 9, 1874, the clanging of the fire bell awakened Harriet Sanders in her home on Fifth Avenue. From her windows, she could see billows of black smoke coming from the south end of town. Her husband was in Virginia City at court, so she dressed quickly and roused her son, James.

A fierce wind carried sparks in the air, endangering rooftops along Broadway and beyond as mother and son fought through the gusts and red-hot embers. They climbed the hill to the fire tower to get a better view. The flames had crossed Main Street, and the International Hotel was on fire. They scrambled down the hill to the rear entrance of the St. Louis Hotel, raced down the hotel stairs and entered Main Street. Harriet later wrote in her reminiscence, *Biscuits and Badmen,* that signs and awnings were falling as the wind fanned the flames. The Holter and Hedges Building was as yet unscathed, and they made their way up the stairs to her husband's law office. A passerby kicked in the locked door. As flames encroached, Harriet had to decide what to save: her husband's papers and files, his law books, the Historical Society's collections or the public library. She and James could not carry many books, so Harriet took off her shawl, laid it on the floor and ordered James to retrieve all the papers in her husband's desk. A stranger appeared and offered to carry the shawl, which contained some three bushels of papers. As flames burned their faces, the three escaped.

The Canyon Ferry stage driver later remarked that he knew Helena was on fire. The wind carried burning shingles fifteen miles out of town. The fire consumed the Holter and Hedges Building and its contents, as well as an additional 150 buildings. It did $850,000 (approximately $2.5 million in modern currency) in personal property damage. The effects were far reaching. The Montana Historical Society's vast newspaper collection today lacks first runs of some of Montana's early issues due to this fire.

The public library hardly missed a beat, retrieving its books on loan to serve as the core collection. The library then moved into rooms on Broadway, sharing space with the territorial law library. Miss Lou Guthrie served as librarian of both. In 1883, territorial legislation allowed communities to form free public libraries. The Helena library continued, however, to charge subscription fees. As the two libraries outgrew their rented rooms, the territory built the Alden Block—which still stands—on Courthouse Square for its law library. The public library moved with it.

Helena established Montana's first free public library by popular vote in 1886. The Helena Library Association turned over its 2,000 books, and the library moved to the second floor of the Broadwater-Ashby Block at Sixth and Main (where the U.S. Bank Building is today), dispensing with its $5 annual membership fee. By 1890, the library had nearly 5,000 books and circulated 36,526. Miss Guthrie was promoted to state librarian, and other early public librarians included Minnie Slaughter, Leslie Sulgrove (removed in 1892 because "his manners were not agreeable" to patrons) and F.C. Patton.

In 1892, the Helena Public Library got its first separate home adjacent to the Public Auditorium at Seventh and Warren. The two-thousand-pound cornerstone—containing a copper box filled with many items, including contemporary newspapers, an 1891 high school graduation program, coins, ballots and an 1890 Helena map—was laid in March. The auditorium hosted myriad public events, fairs and even funerals. The auditorium and library shared the block with Helena High, Central School and, after 1908, the Seventh Avenue gym.

By the 1910s, the library again began to outgrow its space and needed refurbishing. The trustees looked to Andrew Carnegie, who had financed Montana libraries in Dillon, Lewistown, Livingston and elsewhere, but they

The Helena Public Library, built in 1892 at Seventh Avenue and Warren Street, was adjacent to the City Auditorium. *From author.*

The Unitarian Church, now Grandstreet Theatre, functioned as the Helena Public Library from 1933 to 1977. *From author.*

were too late—those funds had been expended. Then in 1933, the Unitarian Church at Park Avenue and Lawrence Street generously offered its building to the library. Ellen Dean Child gave $18,000 for its renovation and the addition of a second floor.

In 1962, the stone buffalo that once guarded the entry of the First National Bank (the site of the current Livestock Building) was discovered resting in a field. The historic relic had been cast aside and forgotten after the bank building burned in 1944. Rescued and placed at the library's corner, the buffalo became a treasured mascot. The former church (now Grandstreet Theatre) served as the library until the 1970s when it too became overcrowded.

During 1970s urban renewal, demolition at the south end of Last Chance Gulch opened building space. The Helena library merged with Lewis and Clark County and built the current facility in 1976. In 1977, the library and the iconic buffalo moved to the current location. In 2018, the Lewis and Clark Library celebrated its 150th year serving the community. Although its mission has broadened and its circle has widened to include branches in Lincoln, East Helena and Augusta, as well as a traveling bookmobile, the library at the end of South Last Chance Gulch provides informational, educational, cultural and recreational materials and services. On the site where flames once consumed its predecessor, the Lewis and Clark Library remains the true public heart of the Helena community.

8

RED-LIGHT BUSINESSWOMEN

By Ellen Baumler

A curious pair of adjacent plots in Benton Avenue Cemetery includes two wrought iron fences. One is an elaborate, gated enclosure while the other is less ostentatious. Both plots include broken tombstones. The two women who lie beneath the ground, forgotten in eternal rest, are not quite as anonymous as so many of their peers. Pioneers they were, but not the sort to whom we usually pay homage.

At the twilight of the gold rush, in the late 1870s and early 1980s, Helena was a typical western town with a vigilante past still fresh on the pages of its history. For some, it was a place to make a fortune and build a future, but for others, it was literally a dead end. Among the many facets of fast-growing Helena was its seedy underbelly. Throughout the 1860s, when men dominated the camp, public women—prostitutes—intermingled with the general population. Hundreds, even thousands, of these anonymous women became legendary across the West. They made the rounds of the fledgling camps and made considerable money. They came from all ethnic backgrounds and all walks of life. They seldom used their real names and took up the "profession" for many different reasons.

During the 1870s, as Helena became the territorial capital aspiring to respectability, the territorial legislature tried to outlaw dancing saloons and hurdy gurdy houses, but there were loopholes. Saloons, dance halls and brothels crowded Helena's main thoroughfares. By the mid-1880s, public

Agnes Merrill's elaborate gate at Benton Avenue Cemetery includes the date and her name slightly misspelled. *From Ric Seabrook.*

women, soliciting and using vile language, had become a common nuisance in many Montana communities.

The territorial legislature passed a law enabling communities to regulate illegal activities. This effectively created red-light districts and prompted a system of fines in many Montana towns. In Helena, Ordinance No. 71 made employment of women on Main Street (now Last Chance Gulch) in any capacity in establishments selling intoxicating liquors a misdemeanor. Further, it prohibited houses of ill fame on Main Street north of Bridge Street (now State Street). Fines ranged from $1 to $100.

After 1885, Helena's red-light district assumed more formal boundaries. Cribs—small one-room rentals—and brothels lined Clore Street (now South Park Avenue) roughly from the foot of Reeder's Alley to the current Blackfoot Brewery. Higher-class parlor houses and other establishments spread out on Wood (now Miller) and Joliet Streets where Josephine "Chicago Joe" Hensley's famed Coliseum, Mollie Byrnes's The Castle, Lillie McGraw's place at the foot of the Bluestone House and other houses extended to Warren Street, which served as the boundary line between respectable and red-light neighborhoods.

Urban renewal destroyed all vestiges of the district in the 1970s. Helena's only surviving 1880s brothel, identified as "female boarding" on historic Sanborn-Perris Fire Insurance maps, is the Caretaker's House, now Cotton Top Bakery, at 212 South Park. The Pioneer Cabin next door is never so identified, but its history during the 1880s and 1890s is suspect.

Federal law closed—or attempted to close—red-light districts during World War I to control the spread of venereal disease among the troops. Women vacated the old places and resurfaced in formerly legitimate hotels and rooming houses. Such places advertising "furnished rooms" became a standard joke. What was furnished went unexplained. Georgia Lee, Pearl Maxwell and Ida Levy were a few of the madams operating on South Main Street from the 1920s. "Big Dorothy" Baker, Ida's successor, was Helena's last madam whose business was at 19½ South Main Street (above the current Windbag Saloon) until 1973.

Public women were not always unwitting victims. While there are many sordid stories, there are also women who chose the work and made a good living. Prostitution occasionally provided a step to marriage and respectability; however, it often led to alcoholism, drug addiction, disease and/or suicide. In the nineteenth century, laudanum, morphine and opium were readily available. Death of an employee or a partner in a madam's house was an occupational hazard.

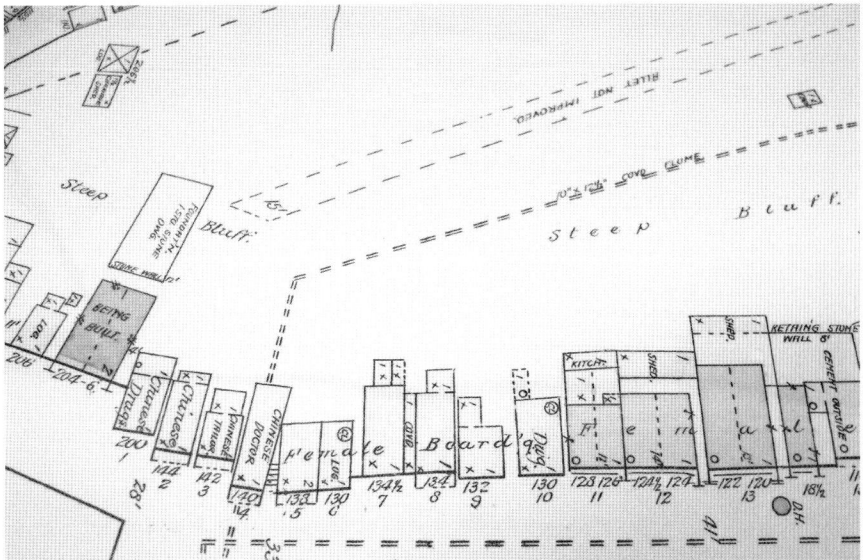

A map of Clore Street documents female boardinghouses intermingled with Chinese businesses. Sanborn-Perris Fire Insurance Map of Helena, 1890. *From MHS Research Center.*

Newspapers offered details. Mrs. Martha "Dutch Lena" Hughes, for example, died of an overdose at Josephine Hensley's Wood Street house. Martha was intoxicated when she took 120 doses, or 15 grains, of morphine that were purchased at a local drugstore. Minnie Gadden mixed morphine and whiskey and died suddenly at her house on Clore Street. There was no inquest because, as the *Herald* reported on June 3, 1875, morphine overdose was the cause, whether by design or by mistake. Kitty Williams, at twenty-six, was proprietress of a house in partnership with Mabell Hall on the corner of Bridge and Joliet. She tried to break her opium habit with small amounts of morphine and overdosed in December 1886. Likewise, Sadie Dean overdosed on morphine at the house of Blanche Emerson in 1885.

Blanche Emerson was a well-known Helena madam whose real name was Carrie Patterson. Her path was set at nineteen in 1870 when she was an inmate at New York City's Mercy House for troubled girls and women. By 1880, she worked in Helena as a prostitute. In 1884, Emerson purchased a house on Clore Street. When she died in 1889, there was no record of her death, only the *Independent Record's* October 19, 1889 notice that her will was in probate. She was thirty-eight.

Like Emerson, frontier prostitutes frequently died young from undocumented causes. The two women buried in the Benton Avenue plots fall into this category. They, however, left unusually detailed records because they owned substantial property and died intestate. The probate records of Frances "Fannie" Spencer and Agnes Merrill provide a tiny, unique glimpse into their private lives.

Fannie Spencer, the daughter of a frontier Mormon family, married Isaac Fordonski in 1865. The couple settled in Virginia City, Montana Territory. In May 1867, Isaac discovered Fannie in bed with Barney Hughes, one of the Alder Gulch discovery men. Affidavits in the 1871 Gallatin County divorce proceedings include witnesses who testified to Fannie's life as a prostitute in Helena. She made substantial income and died at thirty-six in 1881 at her Bridge Street house—one of two she owned. She left an estate valued at approximately $6,000 ($48,000 in modern currency).

The inventory and sale of Fannie's assets filed in probate court reveal clues about her lifestyle and associations. Among her unpaid bills were several hundred dollars in doctors' fees and pharmacy expenses, suggesting an acute illness. To satisfy her debts, estate administrators held a public sale of Fannie's personal property. The list of items and buyers provides tantalizing information. Among the chairs, tables, spittoons, curtains

Pineapples, a symbol of hospitality, adorn the iron fence around Agnes Merrill's gravesite. *From author.*

and kitchenware sold were parlor and chamber sets, an oval mirror and a center table purchased by Josephine Hensley. Blanche Emerson purchased a chandelier, a cream pitcher, wine glasses and goblets. Helena businessman Michael Reinig purchased fifty-seven yards of carpet. From the sale proceeds, $901.61 went to pay creditors. Fannie's mother and three siblings in Salt Lake City received the remaining $378.39.

Brief notices of the death of Agnes Merrill (known as Belle Flynn) on December 8, 1878, also give no hint about the cause. A lack of medical bills might suggest that death was swift. In partnership with Lillie McGraw (who rose to wealth but died of cirrhosis of the liver in 1898), Lillie was the highest bidder and purchased Agnes's half interest in the house and its contents, including chairs, tables, lamps, bedding, carpets and cuspidors.

The list of clothing and jewelry in a trunk sent to Agnes's mother and sister in Springfield, Illinois, is poignant. Among the items are a mink cloak, an ermine muff and collar, a black velvet cloak, silk dresses, a black alpaca suit and other suits, a corset and undergarments, two pairs of shoes, a fine gold buckle, a breast pin and eardrops. These give some idea of Agnes's expensive possessions and fancy clothing. One wonders what her family made of it.

The graves of Fannie Spencer and Agnes Merrill symbolize many women who headed west with hope for a better life. These two enjoyed brief prosperity that ended all too soon. Agnes's unusual fence memorializes her and speaks to the person we might assume she was. The gate, indelibly painted and beautifully personalized, displays her misspelled name. Pineapples, the southern symbol of hospitality, cap the wrought iron fence posts, suggesting that visitors are most welcome.

9

TROUBLE WITH NEIGHBORS

The House of the Good Shepherd

By Ellen Baumler

The National Register–listed House of the Good Shepherd Historic District is a curious collection of buildings that wrap around the corner of Ninth Avenue and Hoback Street. The complex includes an attractive French Second Empire residence (now apartments) with a long-abandoned brick chapel attached and a spacious dormitory (now the studio of sculptor Tim Holmes) next door to the south. A tall board fence, shielding inmates from prying eyes, once surrounded the buildings that seem oddly out of place among the neighborhood's modest homes. Because of its mission and its inmates, the complex has a dark history.

The mission of the Order of the Good Shepherd was primarily to rehabilitate prostitutes by providing a safe, healthy environment with virtuous role models, but it also included wayward and reformatory children. The order came from France to the United States in the 1840s.

By the 1880s, Helena was a progressive regional center of Catholic services, including medical, social and educational institutions. The Most Reverend John B. Brondel, the first bishop of Helena, viewed mining camps like Helena as wicked places where many women needed reforming. He also feared young girls, especially, could be enticed into unhealthy activities. What better, more progressive service could the church perform than to offer a refuge and a new beginning? At the bishop's invitation, five Sisters of the Good Shepherd arrived from Saint Paul, Minnesota, in 1889. The nuns settled into the convent built for them at Ninth and Hoback.

The sisters' 1890s chapel abuts the sisters' convent—now apartments—at Hoback Street and Ninth Avenue. *From author.*

The sisters' success was immediate. In 1890, the completed two-story frame dormitory increased capacity, and soon after, the town's second Catholic church, Saint Helena's across the street at 449 North Hoback, was formally dedicated. The white-robed sisters became a frequent sight in the neighborhood. Even though some neighbors disliked the unsavory element in residence and believed that inmates were imprisoned under lock and key, neighbors had no real reason to complain. That, however, was soon to change. The *Helena Journal* reported in detail on volatile events that erupted in the neighborhood in April 1892.

At the center was fourteen-year-old Linnie Connor, whose story played out partly behind the board fence, partly in a Helena courtroom and ultimately ended in tragedy. It began when neighbors witnessed Mrs. Connor, Linnie's stepmother, forcibly ejecting the teenager from their home in the 900 block of Eighth Avenue. Linnie fled to the Fifth Avenue home of grocer Emil Wommelsdorf. The next day, the Connors went to collect her. As neighbors watched in horror, her parents carried her out, "choking and gagging her to stifle her screams." They dragged her down Hoback Street to the House of the Good Shepherd, where Mother Superior Mary Margaret reluctantly accepted Linnie. Three Helena papers carried the story.

Another neighbor later reported hearing Linnie's muffled crying on the other side of the fence, and when a passerby climbed to peer over it, an inmate yelled an obscenity. Neighbors were appalled that Linnie's father would force an innocent child into the midst of "fallen" women and were aghast that the sisters would take in a young girl of spotless character. A group of ladies went to see the mother superior to demand Linnie's release, but Mother Mary Margaret refused to surrender her. The *Journal* editorialized that the sisters' "dirty work" was one thing, but Christian women could not stand by and watch the mistreatment of one's own child.

Hours passed as neighbors worked themselves into a frenzy. They marched to the Connors' house and erected a makeshift effigy of Linnie's father, pinning a note to it that said: "C. Connor—Made His Child Homeless." Upon the front sidewalk, someone chalked the vigilante warning: "3-7-77."

Linnie's parents removed her from the home the following morning and placed her with friends. Bishop Brondel responded to the *Journal's* accusations in a letter to the *Daily Independent*, assuring the public that the home was neither a prison nor "merely a reformatory to reclaim the fallen but also a school of preservation to guard young people against danger." The bishop further charged that leaving a child at the Good Shepherd would leaven no stain but rather place her under proper guardianship and discipline. The bishop maintained that the sisters were legally and morally bound to first accept the girl and then to surrender her only to her legal guardian. To say that the sisters violated Christian charity by taking Linnie into the house "is not the saying of a sane man."

A few days later, Linnie suffered a "serious nervous attack" when she discovered that her father planned to send her to an institution. Linnie's friends engaged the services of Ella Knowles, the state's first female attorney. Knowles, who ran for state attorney general a few months later and lost, was building up her reputation. She gladly accepted the well-publicized case, collected a dozen or more affidavits, roused District Court Judge Buck and obtained a restraining order on Charles Connor, duly served at 10:30 p.m. Saturday. Among the witnesses was Dr. Napoleon Salvail, who stated that Linnie had a condition "approaching epilepsy," aggravated by her father's beatings and unsettled circumstances.

The courtroom was packed when the judge heard Linnie's petition asking for the appointment of a guardian. Linnie and a dozen friends and neighbors testified. Few were sympathetic to the parents, who claimed Linnie had become uncontrollable and that they had done what they thought best. Judge Buck then made his ruling. Mr. Connor was placed under the court's supervision and ordered not to lay a hand on his daughter, send her away or force her to go anywhere against her will without the court's consent. Court proceedings were dismissed when Linnie was placed in the home of a family friend, satisfying all parties.

During the next few months, Linnie re-established a good relationship with her parents. Then her health gave way and Dr. Salvail diagnosed a brain tumor. She returned to her parents' home and died peacefully in October. Consulting doctors agreed that the tumor caused drastic changes in her behavior.

The sisters continued their work. In 1900, nine sisters had charge of twenty-seven inmates—three over the age of thirty; the youngest was eight. By 1904, the dormitory had been enlarged four times, and the home operated a commercial laundry facility, providing income and job training for residents. However, working in the stifling, windowless basement was brutal.

No one complained when the home moved to a new two-hundred-bed facility west of town in 1909. The home occasionally attracted the press. There was a spectacular episode in 1913 when wealthy Thomas Cruse

The House of the Good Shepherd's dormitory on Hoback Street between Eighth and Ninth Avenues housed women and girls until 1909. *From author.*

A few graves remained at Calvary Cemetery when this photo was taken circa 1989. The area now lies under a residential neighborhood. *From Dundee Warden.*

brought his gravely ill daughter, Mamie, to the home. Three times married and divorced, and an alcoholic, Mamie was an inmate for some weeks. When the sisters released her to the care of her father, she died a few days later. The cause on her death certificate was Bright's disease—a catch-all kidney ailment. But there was valid speculation on the true nature of her illness and whether she had been under the sisters' care against her will.

The House of the Good Shepherd became an accredited school accepting "girls endangered by vicious surroundings and those inclined to evil nature." The home established Calvary Cemetery on the property, where sisters and lay persons were buried from 1910. The sisters cultivated reciprocity with the nearby Florence Crittenton Home, and although the sisters accepted no pregnant girls, burial records show that at least one newborn was buried at the home's cemetery as late as the 1950s. There were others—officially unrecorded—marked with metal tags. Clearly, the sisters continued their mission to offer the wayward a haven. During seventy-eight years in Helena, more than twenty-seven hundred young women and girls benefited from the sisters' care.

The home, along with other Catholic institutions in Helena, closed in 1967. The sprawling facility at the end of Flowerree Street was demolished in 1969. Most, but not all, graves in Calvary Cemetery were removed to Resurrection Cemetery in 1968. Helena residents recall remnant graves that were not moved when residences were built over the area. Only the home's former gymnasium, now Saint Andrew School, stands today.

10

Was Helena Invaded by Hairy Aliens in 1976?

By Jon Axline

Something very weird happened to a high school sophomore in the Helena Valley in 1976. Bob Lea, a Capital High student and member of the school's wrestling team, lived in a two-story house on Hickman Drive, near the junction of Canyon Ferry and York Roads, with his parents and sister. The house still exists and has a spectacular view of the Spokane Hills and an open irrigated farm field to the east. Just before five in the morning on Sunday, April 4, Lea woke and looked out his second-floor window onto the open field. He hadn't put on his glasses but could see well enough in the partial darkness to spot something unusual walking across the field east of his house—a very large something.

Lea quickly retrieved his glasses and was immediately spooked because "it wasn't someone, it was something." He watched the creature walk north across the field to a haystack about 250 yards from his house. There it met a second creature that was much shorter than the first. Both creatures appeared about the same—hairy with "little or no neck." At the haystack, both creatures examined what appeared to be some kind of device. Lea described it as "a lot bigger than a bale of hay with something sticking out of it like a handle." After a couple minutes the creatures started walking toward his house.

The teenager later told *Independent Record* reporter Gene Fischer that he "really didn't realize just how big they were until the large one walked by two posts in the field that are about eight feet tall. It was much taller than

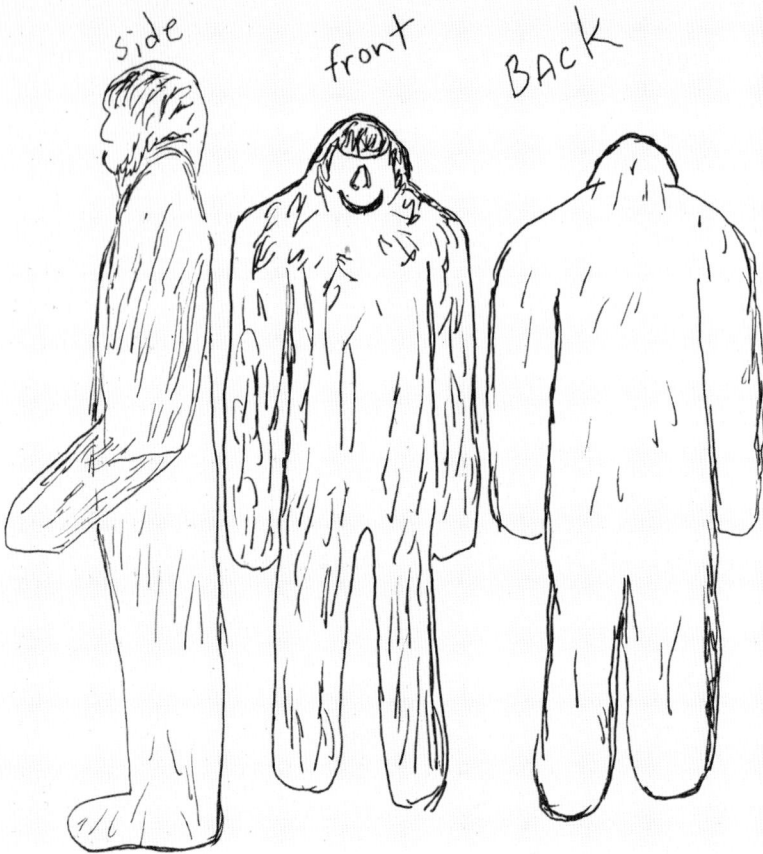

Bigfoot witness Bob Lea provided a rough sketch of the creatures for investigators in 1976. *From Roberta Donovan and Keith Wolverton's* Mystery Stalks the Prairie.

the posts; I would guess that the creature stood about ten feet tall." When the creatures reached the posts, which were about eighty-five feet from his house, Lea was "really getting shook by then" and ran downstairs to tell his father, Bob Sr. As it was early on a Sunday morning, it took a while to rouse his dad out of bed. By the time Mr. Lea got out of bed and took a look out the window, the creatures were gone.

That morning, Lea's mother convinced her son to report the incident to the sheriff's department. Two deputies soon arrived, took the boy's statement and searched the field for evidence of the otherworldly visitors.

They found none. The deputies wrote the whole thing off as "the vivid imagination of a young boy."

Maybe that should have been the end of it, but it wasn't. The day following the incident, Lea's little sister, Debbie, was scouring the field, looking for evidence to support her brother's claim, and she found something. She discovered three huge tracks in the field, seeming to bolster Bob's claim about the creature's extraordinary height and long stride. Because it was late in the day when Debbie found the tracks, she covered them and returned the next day to make plaster casts of them. Only one was usable, and it revealed that there truly may have been something odd in the field that Sunday morning. The plaster cast showed a footprint seventeen inches long and seven inches wide. The print indicated that the creature had three toes, with the middle toe being longest, and it was decidedly not human.

After the article about the sighting appeared in the *Independent Record*, it's hard to imagine the amount of teasing Bob Lea suffered in the halls of Capital High. But his story seemed plausible enough to draw the attention of Cascade County sheriff Keith Wolverton. He paid a visit to Lea at his home on Hickman Drive. The sheriff had been fielding reports of UFOs, hairy giants and cattle mutilations for several months. Unlike his colleagues, Wolverton tended to give witnesses the benefit of the doubt after reporting what they'd seen. Later that year, he and Lewistown newspaper correspondent Roberta Donovan published a book, *Mystery Stalks the Prairie*, that detailed their investigations into those baffling occurrences.

Wolverton believed the plaster cast was genuine and concluded that Bob Lea was telling the truth about what he saw in the field east of his house. The sheriff told the *Independent Record* that there had been fourteen reports of hairy creatures called into his office after he made an appeal for information in February. The latest sighting just happened to involve an East Helena resident.

On the morning of February 22, Leonard Hegele, a twenty-nine-year-old Helena Vo-Tech (now Helena College) student was driving south on Interstate 15, just south of the Great Falls International Airport interchange. He and his wife and two children were headed home to East Helena after spending the weekend visiting relatives in Conrad. He spotted a seven-foot-tall, "solid and muscular" creature striding along a knoll on the north side of the interstate about a quarter mile from the highway. He stopped the car, crawled through the right-of-way fence,

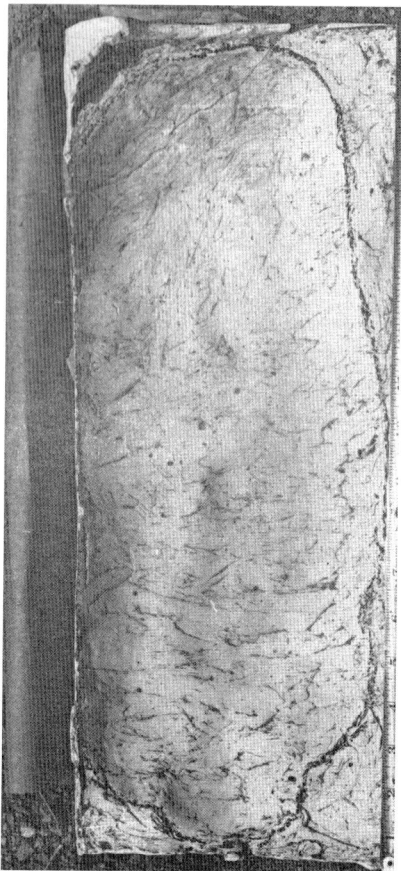

Debbie Lea made a plaster cast of a footprint made by one of the creatures. *From Roberta Donovan and Keith Wolverton's* Mystery Stalks the Prairie.

crossed the frontage road and began chasing the creature, who didn't seem too concerned about its pursuer, though Hegele was toting a .357 magnum pistol. When Hegele got within about 750 feet of the entity, the creature stopped and turned to face him. At that point, Hegele lost his nerve and skedaddled back to his car and family. As he turned to run, Hegele noticed an oval object hovering not far from the humanoid. The creature made no menacing gestures toward its pursuer, and Hegele was unsure if it was covered in hair like other reported creatures at the time.

Undoubtedly, something strange was happening in the Helena and Great Falls areas in the mid-1970s, but what that was is still a mystery. The *Great Falls Tribune* and the *Independent Record* made plenty of references to the myriad sightings of strange creatures. Most people, however, felt that the hairy entities were nothing more than frolicking hippies and not something from outer space. One Great Falls couple, who went by the names of Chris and Dove, even told a newspaper reporter that they were waiting to board a flying saucer for transport to outer space and eternal life. Sheriff Wolverton took the sightings seriously enough to travel to Helena to interview one young witness.

This author, while employed at Buttrey's at the time of the incident, remembers the rumors of frightened residents in the area. We'll never know what Bob Lea saw—if anything—but it sure makes for a ripping good yarn and addition to Helena's hidden history.

II

THE HANGING OF THE
GOLDEN LANTERNS

Nighttime Airway Beacons Surround the Capital City

By *Jon Axline*

Helena residents no doubt have seen the lights flashing from mountaintops surrounding the valley. At regular intervals they flickered a white, then red. There was, and is, a certain comfort in the steady flash and the fact that they've been doing it for as long as many residents can remember. The flashing lights are taken for granted now, but they were once a really big deal and marked a significant milestone in the advancement of aviation in the United States, making the country a worldwide leader in the industry. The beacon lights allowed—for the first time in the nation—air navigation across the continent at night.

Lighted beacons to aid nighttime air navigation were common in the United States from 1923 to the 1960s. At the peak in 1941, 1,550 beacon lights marked airway routes across the country. Montana was integrated into the system in 1931 when the U.S. Department of Commerce's Bureau of Air Commerce installed the first beacon tower at Armstead in southwestern Montana. The big push for a coast-to-coast lighted nighttime airway route for commercial and airmail traffic began in 1934 with the federal designation of the Northern Transcontinental Airway Route between Minneapolis and Seattle.

The Bureau of Air Commerce erected the first beacon towers on the Montana segment of the Northern Transcontinental Airway Route in October 1934, at Miles City. Work in the west began near Lookout Pass in February 1935. Like the Northern Pacific Railway more than half a century before, the bureau planned the two ends to meet somewhere in the middle. Work crews under the supervision of bureau engineer Art Watson began working on six beacon towers between Bozeman and Helena in late July 1935. By mid-September, they had installed all six towers, including the one on top of Spokane Hill, east of Helena and visible from the city. Five beacon towers spanned the ninety air miles between Missoula and Helena, including the last tower to be erected on MacDonald Pass. When lit, the beacon would be the final lamp in a long string of beacons that stretched between Minneapolis and Seattle.

The Bureau of Air Commerce designed the towers in the early 1930s. Engineers determined the sites for the towers—both from air reconnaissance and from the ground. The engineers also supervised the creation of the towers. Each construction crew consisted of twenty-four men. Because the project was federally funded and occurred during the Great Depression, the bureau hired the laborers from local National Re-Employment Service offices. Each crew was made of locals on the unemployment rolls. They each received a minimum wage and worked only thirty-two hours per week. Payment was strictly in cash. Construction included not just the beacon tower but also an accompanying prefabricated steel shed that held the generator that powered the revolving beacon light.

Developed by J.B. Bartow, the beacon lamps consisted of million-candle-power lamps with twenty-four-inch mirror reflectors. The flashing lights were reportedly visible for at least fifteen miles. The lights revolved every tenth of a second. When a bulb burned out, a mechanism automatically replaced it with a new bulb. Along with the revolving beacons, red course lights marked the airway route and flashed a Morse code signal that identified the beacon. The Bureau of Air Commerce built beacon tower sites every ten to fifteen miles across the state. Towers ranged in height from fifteen to ninety-one feet and were topped by seven-foot square steel platforms upon which the beacon lights sat.

Each beacon was, at first, powered by a self-starting generator housed in a shack near the tower. The gasoline-powered generator was self-starting and fueled by a 515-gallon tank that needed filling every eight months. If the main generator failed, a backup took its place. An astronomical clock or a photocell told the generator when to turn the beacon on and off. Ideally, federal "mechanicians" conducted maintenance at each remote beacon site every two weeks. Later, most of the beacons received electricity directly from power lines, but the Strawberry Butte beacon in Gallatin County relied on its generator until 1987.

The MacDonald Pass beacon was the last to be erected on the Northern Transcontinental Airway Route in November 1935. *From author.*

The Civil Aeronautics Authority lit the last beacon on the Northern Transcontinental Airway on MacDonald Pass on November 10, 1935. Twelve days later, on November 22, Helena held its Lighting of the Golden Lantern celebration to mark the completion of the beacon system. Less than a month after two earthquakes devastated the city, around four thousand people braved frigid weather at the Helena Municipal Airport to witness the inauguration of night flight of Northwest Airlines from the Twin Cities to the coast. Attendees heard speeches by local officials, including Fred B. Sheriff, chairman of the Helena Airport Commission, and Eugene Vidal, director of the Bureau of Air Commerce. With considerable exaggeration, Northwest Airlines general manager Croil Hunter lauded "the rays of the beacons point to the greatest development in aviation." The beacons were certainly a major advance in the development of nighttime air navigation but maybe not to the level Hunter claimed.

Helena was at the junction of two national airway routes. National Parks Airway began at Salt Lake City and ran north to Great Falls. Established by the National Parks Airline in 1928, the U.S. Department of Commerce didn't install beacon lights to mark the route until 1934. The Bureau of Air Commerce installed ten beacons every ten to fifteen miles between Dell in Beaverhead County and Helena in 1935. The Helena Chamber of Commerce celebrated the completion of the system to the Queen City on December 20, when a plane full of federal officials, airline executives and Butte dignitaries flew to the Helena airport. There, Helena Chamber of Commerce and airport officials treated them to "an informal smoker at the Montana Club's Rathskeller before they reboarded the plane and flew back to Butte." The *Montana Standard* reported that "ten minutes out of Helena, Butte's multi-colored Christmas raiment of dazzling lights stood out in bold relief in the darkness ahead and shortly after the National Parks' first official night flight had been completed."

It was another two years before the federal government completed the lighted system to Great Falls. In late August 1937, the Bureau of Air Commerce began installation of five beacon towers between Helena and Great Falls. Each were identical in design and function to those on the east to west route. The Stony Point beacon began flashing across the Helena Valley from the north hills in the fall. The beacon overlooked the Gates of the Mountains to the east and the Sleeping Giant to the west. The air commerce bureau completed the National Parks Airway beacon system in December 1937. An observer standing at the Helena Municipal Airport

Federal authorities erected the Stoney Point beacon in the north hills on the National Parks Airway Route in September 1937. *From author.*

could theoretically see beacons flashing from Spokane Hill, Stony Point, Boulder Hill and MacDonald Pass.

The national beacon system reached its zenith in 1941 and then began a slow decline. In 1947, the Civil Aeronautics Authority, which took over from the Bureau of Air Commerce in 1938, decommissioned the non-airport beacons in eastern Montana. By 1965, the Federal Aviation Administration operated only thirty-nine of the original eighty-four Montana beacons. In 1971, the agency made plans to decommission the remaining beacon lights under its jurisdiction and turned over operation of the remaining beacons to the state. The Montana Aeronautics Commission assumed control of the beacons and turned a few off, including the beacon on Boulder Hill in 1984. Attempts to decommission the system in the 1990s failed. By the early twenty-first century, Montana was the last state to operate and maintain nighttime airway beacons. Many of these historic relics are now privately owned and maintained. The Stony Point, Spokane Hill and Macdonald Pass beacons still stand as reminders of the golden age of American aviation and continue to shine out against Montana's big sky.

12

THEY SHALL NOT PASS

The Ground Observer Corps and the Helena Filter Center

By Jon Axline

For seven years during the 1950s, Helena was on the front line of the Cold War. Even before the end of World War II in 1945, tensions had mounted between the United States and the Soviet Union. The disparate political systems were incompatible with each other, and meaningful peace seemed hopeless. Nuclear weapons intensified the problems, especially after the Soviets exploded their own atomic bomb in 1949 and the Korean War erupted in 1950. The Cold War was marked by escalating rhetoric and mounting military tension. The establishment of civil defense organizations, propaganda, McCarthyism and anxiety at home were the hallmarks of the era for most Americans. National defense and the fear of a nuclear Pearl Harbor were big issues in the lives of Helenans. In the early 1950s, the U.S. Air Force was successfully able to couple its military goals with civilian angst by forming the Ground Observer Corps (GOC).

It was a simple system: civilians manning observation posts watched the skies for aircraft. When spotted, the observers noted the approximate altitude of the bogie and the direction it was flying. They then phoned the sighting in to designated filter centers where other volunteers under air force supervision plotted them on map boards until the object could be identified. If they remained unidentified, the air force scrambled fighter jets to intercept them. In July 1951, the air force kicked off Operation Skywatch to formally activate the GOC.

The air force relied on posters to attract volunteers to the Ground Observer Corps. They appealed to family instincts and protecting Americans from communism. *From author.*

There were two filter centers (FC) in Montana—one in Billings and the other in Helena. The Helena FC was initially located on the second floor of the old high school building on North Warren Street. The center consisted of a horizontal plotting board and a bank of telephones staffed by civilian volunteers under the supervision of an air force officer and fourteen airmen. The Helena FC was responsible for sixty-five thousand square miles of western and central Montana and around forty-five hundred volunteers in the observation posts. The filter center operated on a "training and standby basis" until May 1952, when the Continental Air Defense's 4773rd Ground Observer Squadron officially activated it. When activated, the center claimed three hundred volunteers and one hundred trainees. Each volunteer worked a four-hour shift—the center was supposed to be open twenty-four seven.

Through its existence, though, the filter center was chronically short of volunteers. Articles and advertisements seeking volunteers frequently appeared in the *Independent Record*. The air force sponsored bimonthly open houses to entice citizens to volunteer and showed propaganda films at noontime civic club luncheons. A Ground Observer Corps Week occurred every spring in another effort to draw volunteers into the fold. The campaigns appealed to personal patriotism and national security, and it was indoor work—unlike the outdoor observation posts. The air force held biannual dinners in which it presented the volunteers with wings, badges and certificates of merit for hours served in the filter center. Despite the efforts put into the campaigns, they enjoyed only limited success, and the lack of volunteers was a persistent problem.

Most of the volunteers at the Helena FC, and, indeed nationally, were middle-class housewives and teenagers. Most of the teenage volunteers did so as part of social organizations or because of peer pressure. Although the Girl Scouts and Campfire Girls supplied most of the volunteers, a fair number of teenage boys also served at the FC—perhaps to do their patriotic duty and meet girls. Mrs. Francis Scholefield was the first civilian administrator of the center and did much to organize it in 1951. Aileen Decker took over as civilian administrator of the FC in September 1951 and remained in that position until the filter center closed in December 1957. During her six years of skywatcher service, she logged more than seven thousand volunteer hours. She was assisted by Dorothy Lay, Ruth Lieberg and Jan Palmquist, who also put in an incredible number of hours at the center. Esther Smith edited the filter center's mimeographed newsletter, the *Minute Man*. Adults and teenagers also assisted in recruiting new volunteers, gave presentations for local civic groups and hosted open houses.

Though recruiting posters made it appear that skywatching was glamorous and exciting, it was more often mundane, especially if no airplanes were spotted. *From author.*

By 1956, it became apparent to the air force that the quarters in the high school were no longer adequate. The long, narrow stairways made accessing the second floor of the high school a problem for many older volunteers, as were the cramped filter center room and the lack of amenities. Air force captain Don Beck brokered a deal with the board of directors of the Montana Club to occupy a space on the fourth floor of its building at Sixth and Fuller. The room, which had previously been used for banquets and receptions, proved ideal for the GOC. It allowed "darkened room" procedures, space for a new vertical plotting board, "the latest communication equipment available" and easy access with twin elevators.

The new filter center opened for business on November 15, 1956. The center's volunteers and staff hosted four hundred visitors at the facility's open house. Volunteers walked the visitors through the Skywatch process, explained the GOC's importance to national defense and served refreshments to what they hoped were potential volunteers. Montana governor J. Hugo Aronson and air force general Harold Neely, commander of the Twenty-Ninth Air Division at Malmstom Air Force Base, officially opened the filter center.

The air force intended the GOC to be temporary until improvements in continental early warning radar systems developed enough to make the organization unnecessary. The military reached that point in April 1957. The deployment of the Mid-Canada and Distant Early Warning (DEW) lines effectively made the sky watchers obsolete. The air force placed much of the organization on ready reserve status, meaning it would only be

Volunteers supervised by air force personnel mapped the path of the bogies on large plotting tables. *From* Helena Independent Record, *March 9, 1952.*

activated in time of national emergency. In December 1957, the military closed the Helena FC and consolidated its operations with the Billings FC. At a farewell banquet 175 GOC volunteers listened to speeches by General Neely and Governor Aronson. Of those, 66 volunteers, including the indefatigable Aileen Decker, received their last awards from the air force.

While short lived, the Helena FC played an important role in national defense during the Cold War. It is not known how many phone calls it fielded from the observation posts, but the center was active in the community. In August 1953, Continental Air Defense Command named the Helena center one of the top four in the Central Air Defense Force. Once an important part of the Helena community, the presence of the filter center and its importance to the national defense during the Cold War is nearly forgotten.

13

PLANTING THE SEEDS OF SAINT PETER'S HOSPITAL

By Ellen Baumler

Montana's Episcopal missionary bishop Leigh Brewer met with his vestry in 1883 to establish a Protestant hospital in Helena. Painfully cognizant of the Roman Catholics' efforts to build Montana institutions, he was especially concerned that Helena's Protestant population had no alternative to the Catholic Saint John's Hospital. As plans for the hospital took root, it became clear that although men made up the board of trustees, church women did the real work. They not only took care of the health of patients but also helped secure the hospital's financial base. Many Helena women contributed in myriad ways to this important cause, but there are four who stand out as the cornerstones upon which Saint Peter's Hospital rests. Bishop Brewer's wife, Henrietta; Mrs. Anton (Mary Pauline) Holter; Georgia C. Young; and Dr. Maria Dean planted the seeds that continue to grow.

The year 1883 was pivotal to Helena's permanence like no other year past or future. It was in this year that the Northern Pacific Railroad steamed into a makeshift depot in Helena's Sixth Ward, where city fathers envisioned a new city center would emerge. The railroad's presence was more than a convenience—it linked the capital city to the outside world and assured its stability. It was on the cusp of this great event that Saint Peter's took root.

Henrietta Brewer embraced the hospital crusade. She and her circle of friends began systematically canvassing for funds. The first donations and supplies came from the Women's Auxiliary of the Episcopal Diocese of Connecticut. The first hospital was near the busy depot in a small house donated by Mrs. S.J. Jones, whose husband later financed the Atlas Block. The tiny facility proved too far out of town to serve the community. Less than six months later, Henrietta and her friend Mary Pauline Holter arranged for the hospital to move to the Holters' former home at Jackson and Grand Streets. There were 225 patients that first year, 80 of whom were East Helena smelter workers sick with lead poisoning.

None of the women involved had hospital training. When the supervisors, Dr. R.F. Clark and his wife—both medical doctors—moved their practice to Butte, the hospital was in dire need of professional expertise. Henrietta's fund-raising network led her back to the Connecticut Auxiliary and to Georgia C. Young, a graduate of the nurses training school in New Haven, Connecticut. Henrietta laid out her case, telling Miss Young, "The hospital is without resources and supplies. I do not know that we can pay you even, but the work is great. It is the Master's work, and it must succeed." Georgia Young accepted this challenge and was Helena's first professionally trained nurse. The Connecticut Auxiliary appropriated an annual salary of $400. When Miss Young arrived and saw the frame hospital building, she was appalled at its inadequacy. She later recalled that when she undressed after her first day, she was covered with lice. All the hospital bedding had to be destroyed, and she started over.

At the end of 1885, a diphtheria epidemic claimed the lives of many Helena children, including two daughters of prominent physician Benjamin C. Brooke. During this dark time, Dr. Maria Dean was the newly appointed head of the local board of health. Dr. Dean understood what most others did not: the disease was highly contagious. She ordered that no bedding of diseased people could be aired on sidewalks or in backyards, she placed quarantine flags on houses where diphtheria was present and imposed a five-dollar fine on those who did not observe these orders. The public resented did not understood these extreme measures, but Dr. Dean saved countless lives.

A graduate of the Boston School of Medicine and further trained abroad, Maria Dean endured the prejudice of her male classmates. This made her a compassionate doctor. As a member of Saint Peter's Episcopal Church, Maria soon joined the cause to build a better Protestant hospital. In 1887, Saint Peter's moved to its longtime location at Logan and Eleventh Avenue. The first photographs show the building starkly resting upon tailing piles—a remnant of the gold rush.

St. Peter's Hospital was built on tailing piles at Eleventh Avenue and Logan Street in 1887. *From Parchen Drugs, Helena souvenir, 1891.*

Under the strict supervision of Georgia Young, Saint Peter's struggled to come into its own. Henrietta Brewer and Mary Pauline Holter organized their friends to help. These "lady visitors" included many women from the Helena community. They inspected the facility weekly and did much of the cooking and cleaning. Dreams to build a new wing were unfulfilled when the always energetic Henrietta died of heart failure in 1903. Her friends, however, took over her important work, and an impressive addition designed by renowned architect Cass Gilbert was named for her.

Mary Pauline Holter and Henrietta Brewer made a formidable team. Mary Pauline's special interest was in aiding the poor, especially children, and she and Henrietta complemented each other. When Henrietta died in 1903, Mary Pauline gifted a valuable static machine with an X-ray attachment in memory of her friend. And after Mary Pauline died at seventy-one in 1912, her heirs gave $25,000 for the support of the children's ward.

If Mary Pauline Holter and Henrietta Brewer were the financial administrative wizards, Dr. Maria Dean and Georgia Young formed the hospital's medical backbone. Dr. Dean, the twenty-seventh Montana physician licensed to practice after statehood in 1889, was long associated with Saint Peter's, specializing in the diseases of women and children. In 1900, one-fourth of all children died before age five. Medicine was not so much a science as it was the practice of healing and compassion. At this Maria excelled. She also championed young women and in 1911 was a key founder of the Helena YWCA. As physician and humanitarian, she tirelessly lobbied the Montana legislature to establish a girls' reform school, which came to fruition with the founding of Mountain View in the Helena Valley in 1919. The epitaph on her tombstone at Forestvale Cemetery reads simply, "The Beloved Physician."

Georgia Young was Saint Peter's nursing superintendent until she retired in 1910. She went on to do social work, and in 1915, the city council appointed her Helena's first policewoman—an experimental position. Although she did the job admirably, the council abolished the position in 1918 because it claimed that the community did not have enough work for her.

Georgia Young and Maria Dean were lifelong friends and partnered in business dealings outside the hospital, as well as on difficult medical cases. During Saint Peter's first uncertain decades, when the hospital stood on Logan Street, the two women conspired to adopt a stray mutt that regularly begged at the hospital's kitchen door. They named him Roger,

The Henrietta Brewer Memorial Building (*left*) enlarged the campus. The hospital served at this location until 1968. *From author.*

Saint Peter's nurses' dormitory, now the education center for Saint Paul's Methodist Church, is the only survivor of Saint Peter's first campus. *From author.*

and he captured their hearts. Georgia loved him dearly and made sure the volunteer cooks fed him well. Roger also charmed Dr. Dean, who enlisted her artist friend Mary C. Wheeler to paint his portrait. After the painting was on exhibit in a New York gallery, it came back to Montana, where it hangs today in a hospital hallway. It is a not only a tribute to Roger but also a reminder of the 1890s and the two women who did so much for the early institution.

After 1909, Georgia Young and Mary Wheeler lived with Maria Dean at 626 Benton Avenue. It is a poignant coincidence that Georgia and Maria died of cancer within two days of each other in 1919. Mary, a renowned artist, teacher and legend in her own right, moved to California and died there in 1934.

Saint Peter's conducted a nurses' training school from 1910 to 1933 and weathered fire, earthquakes and financial crises. In 1968, the hospital moved from the Logan Street site to its current Broadway location. The only survivor of the old hospital campus is the nurses' residence, which now serves as the education building of Saint Paul's Methodist Church.

Henrietta Brewer, Mary Pauline Holter, Maria Dean and Georgia Young left legacies to the Helena community. Without their determination, enthusiasm, compassion and dedication, Saint Peter's would not be the modern center of Helena's medical community.

14

UNRAVELING THE MYTHS OF HELENA'S CHINATOWN

By Ellen Baumler

Helena was once one of the most culturally diverse places in the American West. During the early mining camp days, a cacophony of languages along busy streets added to the gold rush excitement. Among the diverse groups were Chinese miners and merchants who numbered nearly 20 percent of Helena's population in 1870. Yet by the mid-1950s, few remained. Chinese homes and businesses fell victim to urban renewal, and time erased their cultural footprint. What drew courageous and adventurous Chinese to Montana, and what happened to them?

Western gold discoveries, first in California and then elsewhere, coincided with desperate times in China. Political upheaval, famine, over-population and the Taiping Rebellion (1850–64) claimed twenty to thirty million lives. Husbands, fathers, sons and brothers left their homes for the American West, hoping to make their fortunes and return to China. These western sojourners were almost exclusively from Taishan (Toisan), a district in Guangdong (Canton) Province. They spoke Taishanese, a distinct Cantonese dialect. Language, customs and discrimination contributed to their isolation.

The federal 1882 Chinese Exclusion Act prohibited Chinese laborers from entry into the United States, facilitating two separate histories of the Chinese in the West. The first, largest group comprised the male laborers who arrived before Chinese exclusion to join the gold rush and later helped lay the tracks of the Northern Pacific across the Northwest. The second, much smaller group—doctors, lawyers, pharmacists and businessmen—were allowed into the United States after 1882 if they could prove professional status. They came to support the laboring class. The two groups had language and culture in common, and until 1944, neither could become naturalized U.S. citizens. Their histories in the West, however, are similar but not the same.

Very few Chinese women journeyed west. Among the 660-plus Chinese population in Helena in 1870, only three were women. Exclusion acts made immigration difficult for wives, families and prospective brides. While competition is often cited as the reasoning behind discriminatory legislation, racial prejudice was the real motivation. After 1909, and until 1953, Montana's anti-miscegenation laws prohibited mixed marriages, and the overwhelmingly male Chinese population could not grow. There were exceptions, of course. The Wongs of Helena and the Chinns of Butte, for example, were engaged in early restaurant and mercantile businesses and had large families. Wong descendants remain in Helena today. But most of Helena's Chinese men either returned to China or grew old and died here without families.

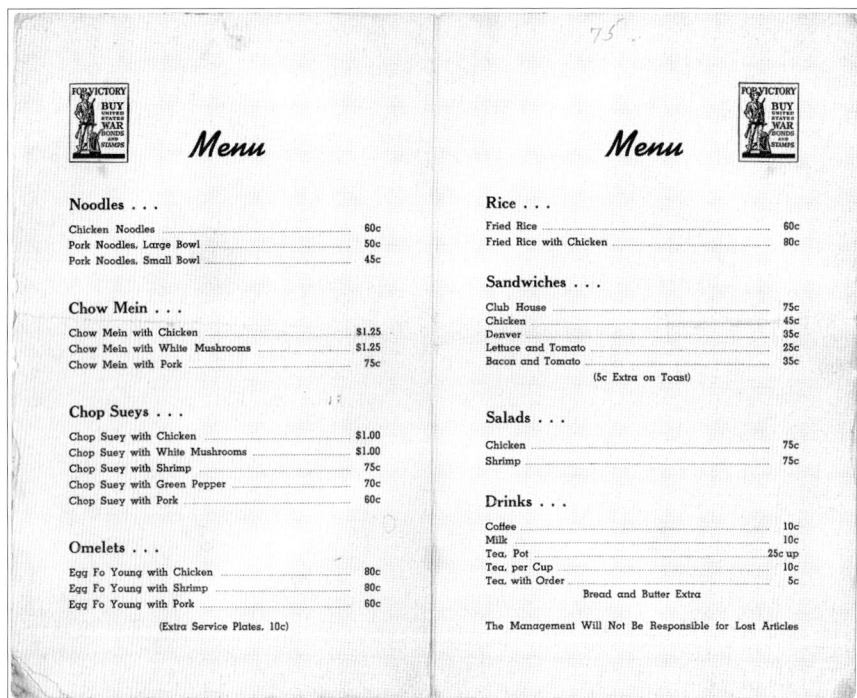

Menu

Noodles . . .

Chicken Noodles	60c
Pork Noodles, Large Bowl	50c
Pork Noodles, Small Bowl	45c

Chow Mein . . .

Chow Mein with Chicken	$1.25
Chow Mein with White Mushrooms	$1.25
Chow Mein with Pork	75c

Chop Sueys . . .

Chop Suey with Chicken	$1.00
Chop Suey with White Mushrooms	$1.00
Chop Suey with Shrimp	75c
Chop Suey with Green Pepper	70c
Chop Suey with Pork	60c

Omelets . . .

Egg Fo Young with Chicken	80c
Egg Fo Young with Shrimp	80c
Egg Fo Young with Pork	60c

(Extra Service Plates, 10c)

Menu

Rice . . .

Fried Rice	60c
Fried Rice with Chicken	80c

Sandwiches . . .

Club House	75c
Chicken	45c
Denver	35c
Lettuce and Tomato	25c
Bacon and Tomato	35c
(5c Extra on Toast)	

Salads . . .

Chicken	75c
Shrimp	75c

Drinks . . .

Coffee	10c
Milk	10c
Tea, Pot	25c up
Tea, per Cup	10c
Tea, with Order	5c
Bread and Butter Extra	

The Management Will Not Be Responsible for Lost Articles

A vintage menu from Yat Son recalls Helena's oldest restaurant, which is still in business under Wong family ownership. *From Fred Wong family.*

China Row, outside the tended grounds of Forestvale Cemetery, holds the remains of perhaps two hundred Chinese Helenans. It was customary to send the bones of those who died on foreign soil back to China. The contracts of Chinese miners or railroad laborers working for companies included insurance promising to return their bones to China should they die on foreign soil. In Helena, as elsewhere, periodic exhumations were done in the nineteenth century. The process, explained in an article in the *Helena Independent Record* on October 14, 1881, included company placer miners meticulously digging the graves, sifting the soil to recover every bone, washing the remains and laying them out to dry. Individual remains were then placed in canvas bags and sent, under guard, to the coast for shipment at a cost of $100 per individual. Some remains in China Row may have been returned to China, but most still lie beneath the windswept prairie. A pile of bricks is all that is left of the traditional funerary burner for the incineration of spiritual tributes such as paper money and clothing. As placer mining dwindled, leaving unskilled laborers stuck in the United States without income, the railroad offered some respite. But for unskilled Chinese immigrants who spoke very little or no English, gardening, laundry and domestic services were areas that provided some opportunities. In 1890, Helena had twenty-six Chinese laundries, and many wealthy families employed Chinese cooks.

Helena's Chinatown stretched roughly from the current Lewis and Clark Library to the south end of town. Typical of other Chinese urban areas, Helena's Chinatown had at least one highly trained physician and a pharmacist/herbalist, as well as various other mercantile shops, groceries and restaurants.

Laundries and gambling and opium-smoking houses were among the first businesses established in most Chinatowns. Chinese people often managed communal opium-smoking rooms. Helena's opium dens, as elsewhere, were not particularly clandestine and were not usually in basements, as often portrayed. One popular opium den, in fact, was next door to the city hall and jail, just south of the current Lewis and Clark Library. Importation of opium to the United States was not illegal until it was banned by federal law in 1909.

Red-light districts and Chinatowns usually intermingled. In Helena, cribs and brothels lined both sides of the street from the foot of Reeder's Alley to 70 South Clore Street (now Park Avenue). Historic Sanborn-Perris Fire Insurance maps label houses of prostitution as *Female Boarding* or *F.B.* and Chinese-occupied buildings as *Chinese*. The relationship between these two

One of the few tombstones surviving at China Row is this 1929 marker. *From Chris Merritt.*

marginalized populations is clear. Women of the district relied on the skilled Chinese herbalists, pharmacists and physicians for birth control, treatment of venereal diseases and opium. Under the care of a physician, opium could produce abortion. In addition, noodle parlors served nutritious, yet inexpensive, meals. Chinese businesses relied on the women's patronage.

Remnant mining tunnels run through many Helena neighborhoods and the area once occupied by Chinatown. However, no remnant tunnels, in Helena or elsewhere, can be attributed exclusively to the Chinese. Likewise, the steam-heating tunnels beneath Helena's downtown are common in most western cities. These tunnels were sometimes used for delivery purposes between businesses, but they were never exclusively used by the Chinese. Sidewalk vaults—lit from above with glass tiles around the Montana Club and elsewhere—served as storage and delivery space. Clandestine use of tunnels exclusively by the Chinese is fiction, not fact.

Stories that Chinese people were forced to live underground is a common myth. However, sometimes basement spaces served as living quarters or boarding houses because the rent was cheap or because space was at a

The altar from Helena's Chinese temple is beautifully symbolic of a land far from the Montana frontier. *From MHS Museum.*

premium. During 1970s urban renewal, bunks reportedly uncovered against the walls in South Main basements most likely served as housing for miners and laborers and not as opium dens.

Finally, stacked rocks, associated with placer tailings and retaining walls like the one behind the Pioneer Cabin, have been labeled "Chinese rock-work." While some walls may have been constructed by Chinese workers, they had no monopoly on stacking rock. Stacked rocks have no cultural footprint.

Chinese sojourners brought Taoist, Buddhist and Confucian beliefs to the American West. In the absence of family homes where altars honored family members, temples in urban Chinatowns substituted. Temples, commonly called joss houses because of the joss sticks, or incense, that patrons burned inside and outside, provided a place to worship and socialize. *Joss* is a Chinese Pidgin English corruption of *deus*, Latin for god.

In Helena and elsewhere, Chinese temples were sometimes called Chinese Masonic Temples. There was no association with Freemasonry, but there were similarities, such as fraternal membership, importance of the number three and elaborate funeral rituals. Association with masons was a way to explain to outsiders the powerful secret structure that controlled its members. The Chinese Six Companies was one of these organizations that contracted and aided immigrant Chinese but also exerted powerful control over them.

The Montana Historical Society's Chinese collection includes an altar from Helena's Chinese Masonic Temple. Its artist/architect is unknown, but the "206 Clore Street" penciled on the bottom hints that its occupant played some role in the altar's creation or installation. From the 1870s to about 1892, that address belonged to a small log cabin next door to the Pioneer Cabin. The cabin is one of several labeled "Chinese."

The altar, richly symbolic of the land left behind, speaks to homesickness and patriotism. The temple was a refuge to these men who kept their customs and beliefs, adapting their lifestyles to the western frontier. Rich green, red and gold paint is typical of Chinese furnishings. Intricate characters flanking the altar's sides, according to translators, poetically glorify a long-dead military hero. Carvings in the wood across the top include silkworm moths fluttering among flowers and pairs of bats, symbolizing good luck.

The altar was a gift in 1973 from Helenan Doris Marshall, who with her husband, Walter, founded the Brewery Theatre in 1954. She purchased the altar at auction, used it in stage productions and then donated it to the Montana Historical Society.

The altar and a stunning embroidered altar cloth are precious few artifacts that help tell the story of Helena's Chinatown. Through research and education, the story of these pioneers is beginning to unfold.

15

THE JOE LOUIS OF THE MAT

The Saga of "King Kong" Clayton

By Jon Axline

Helena has known a lot of colorful characters during its history. Most are long forgotten, but a few, like Tommy Cruse and Myrna Loy, are indelibly associated with the Queen City. Many enjoyed their fifteen minutes of fame as athletes at the baseball park, on the basketball court or in the arena. Sports have played a big role in Helena's history, but some once-popular athletic events have all but disappeared from the Helena sports scene. During the 1930s, the city hosted spirited weekly wrestling exhibitions that drew hundreds of Helena fans to venues around the city to cheer their heroes and hiss their villains. Fifty-five cents bought you an evening of exciting entertainment as grapplers with flamboyant names, like the Red Shadow, Wildcat Pete and Mad Man Otto Ludwig, helped dispel the gloom and doom of the Great Depression. One "rassler," a two-hundred-pound African American named LeRoy "King Kong" Clayton, made a lasting impression on Helena audiences over a twenty-year period beginning in 1937.

Born in Cincinnati, Ohio, in June 1911, LeRoy Clayton attended school in his hometown and in Los Angeles. For a short time, he studied at the University of California–Santa Barbara and Wilberforce University in Zenia, Ohio. While in college, he played football and learned the craft of professional wrestling. After a short stint at graduate school in upstate New York, Clayton joined the ranks of professional wrestlers who were touring the United States. Wrestling under the name of Tiger Jack Nelson, he

Montana wrestling fans and sportswriters counted Clayton among the sport's heroes and complimented his clean style of "rasslin." *From* Helena Independent, *February 19, 1946.*

grappled in his first professional match against Berlo Assirati in Philadelphia in 1928. The referee disqualified Clayton for "rough tactics," but this was the only time he was eliminated from a bout for dirty wrestling. Over the next four years, he was a regular fixture on the wrestling circuit in California, Arizona, Oregon and Utah, before heading north to Montana in the winter of 1937. He began wrestling under the name King Kong Clayton in 1936. In 1932, a sportswriter from Camden, New Jersey, described him as a "veteran who is about as clean as driven snow covered with coal dust."

Clayton's first match in Helena pitted him against Vic Weber, the "Handsome New Yorker," at the recently built Shrine Arena on February 23, 1937. The newspaper was good at promoting the matches each week, but it was less reliable about reporting the results. He wrestled against men with colorful names like Abdul the "Terrible Turk" Kahn, Indian Ike Cazzell, Young Hitler and the Unknown Red Devil. He also grappled with regular joes sporting ordinary names. A short time after his first bout in Helena, it was obvious to his promoter, Tom Alley, that Clayton was popular with the fans. Accordingly, he only arranged matches that pitted Clayton against "villains." Over the years, Clayton earned the sobriquets of Ebony Eraser, the Black Panther and the Colored Flash. According to Clayton, he participated in more than four thousand bouts during his career and won most of them. One of Clayton's biggest fans was *Helena Independent* sportswriter Al Gaskill. His writing style may have influenced long-time Helena radio sports announcer Cato Butler and his lively play-by-plays of high school basketball games.

While the spectators at the matches appeared colorblind, the press was much less so. Wrestling then, as it is today, depended on showmanship to keep the crowds coming back to the arena every week, and the press was good at making stuff up to generate interest in athletes. In Clayton's case, sportswriters in the cities in which he wrestled never failed to mention his race. In a March 1937 newspaper article, Gaskill made it sound like Clayton made all his professional decisions after drinking magic potions and seeking the advice of a "Voodoo Princess." Clayton was a well-educated man, but in the newspapers, his dialect was straight out of *Uncle Tom's Cabin*.

Unlike many wrestlers, Clayton refused to use dirty tactics to defeat his opponents. His favorite move was the flying wristlock, a difficult maneuver at which he excelled. Some bouts were more raucous than others. A particularly rowdy match against the Phantom at the Fox Theatre in Butte in November 1946 ended with both men in the orchestra pit in front of the stage. In February 1932, Al Gaskill described Clayton:

> *Grappler of the first division and many of the boys had found out to their sorrow that he beats them either at straight wrestling or in the more spectacular antics of the mat men. The reason he does not win oftener is his…habit of allowing the other boy to get in plenty of rough stuff and illegal holds and tactics before he cuts loose with even so much as a good solid forearm blow, something absolutely legal in the wrestling game today.*

Clayton reputedly had "middle weights and light heavies backtracking rather than meet him in Montana rings."

Clayton temporarily left the wrestling circuit in 1940 and joined the U.S. Army. He served in a frontline combat engineer battalion and was badly wounded in action while fighting in the Po River Valley of northern Italy in 1945. He earned five battle stars and a Purple Heart with clusters for his actions during the war. After his discharge from the army, Clayton returned to Helena in 1946. He wrestled for a time, but the wounds he received in Italy had somewhat diminished his abilities in the ring.

Prior to a bout in March 1946, Clayton began thrilling audiences with his famous rope trick. The *Independent* reported that the wrestler had a "neck so powerful that he can withstand the pressure of a rope looped around his neck and pulled by ten men on each side." Clayton put this to the test and allowed the men to pull steadily without jerking the ropes. With only a towel around his neck for protection, Clayton could withstand the pressure for up to a minute without being strangled.

Feats of strength, while thrilling to spectators, weren't always successful and almost resulted in disaster. During a match against Chris Zaharias in late March 1946, the two men suffered a head-on collision that knocked both grapplers out for a time. Still groggy from the impact, Clayton demonstrated his famous rope trick afterward and passed out again. It took several minutes to revive him. Despite that scare, Clayton continued to perform the trick for

LET'S GO!

THE EVENT ALL HELENA HAS
BEEN WAITING FOR!

Opening of the Wrestling Season

TONIGHT

8:30 o'Clock

American Legion Hall

WARREN AND GRAND

Featuring a Whirlwind Headline Event

"Duke" Ruppenthal

vs.

King Kong Clayton

Eight 10-Minute Rounds

—————— AND THEN ——————

"Wildcat" Pete vs. Whiskers Adams

Eight 10-Minute Rounds

WITH A SNAPPY OPENER

Art Belcher vs. Klem Kusek

Five 6-Minute Rounds

There Will Be Crowds—So Make Your
Reservations Early! . . . Call 1210-M

RINGSIDE $1.10
Reserved 85c
General Admission 55c

AUSPICES AMERICAN LEGION

In 1937, Clayton appeared at Helena wrestling venues on a weekly basis, grappling with a wide variety of opponents. *From* Helena Independent, *September 13, 1937.*

audiences at the weekly Grunt and Groan Shows at the Shrine Civic Center and for customers at his nightclub.

Maybe because of his age and the wounds he received during the war, Clayton began to cut back a bit on his wrestling career. In April 1946, he opened a nightclub, the Sportsmen's Club, on the second floor of the Exchange Tavern building at 101 South Main Street. The Ebony Eraser promoted the place as an upscale nightspot that featured "Fine Mixed Drinks and bottled beers," nightly dancing and live music. The club's piano player and singer was thirty-three-year-old divorcee Mattie Waite Driver. Clayton's first wife, Thelma, whom he had married in 1932, had recently passed away from acute appendicitis. LeRoy and Mattie married in a civil ceremony in September 1946.

It's difficult to gauge how successful the nightclub was. Certainly, Clayton drew a lot of customers. He hired former and current wrestlers as bartenders and bouncers, including his old nemeses "Roughhouse" George Schnabel and Bud Higgins. For reasons unknown, the nightclub closed in 1947, a little over a year after it opened. Clayton worked at Archie Bray's brickyard for a time before the couple moved to Livingston—Mattie's hometown—with his three daughters from his first marriage. Clayton went to work for the Northern Pacific Railway in 1949, but he continued to wrestle in towns in western Montana, including Helena. He retired permanently from the sport in May 1957, when he "bested One-Hold Jack Domar to the delight and edification of the crowd."

The Clayton family was a popular fixture in Livingston. In addition to working two or three jobs, LeRoy taught wrestling to Livingston's youth, while Mattie provided piano lessons to many. A devoted family man, he was also a keen gardener and an avid fisherman. LeRoy and Mattie were well liked and respected in the Livingston community. Mattie died in April 1975. Thirty-seven days later, LeRoy passed away from a cerebral hemorrhage. For several years, King Kong Clayton was a fixture in the capital city—a well-respected athlete with a large fan base not only in Helena but also in all of western Montana. Unfortunately, his contributions to Helena's sports and entertainment scenes have been largely forgotten.

16

TO ORNAMENT THE CITY

Jewish Landmarks

By Ellen Baumler

Montana's placer gold drew adventurers from every corner of the world and prominent among them were Jewish pioneers. They came from Prussia, Bavaria, Austria and Poland, as well as from San Francisco, New York and Chicago. Opportunity drew these immigrants to the new mining settlements where business and religious beliefs brought them together. Helena is fortunate to have two rare landmarks—the former Temple Emanu-El and the Home of Peace Cemetery—that speak to the optimism and contributions of these important settlers.

On December 9, 1866, Jewish businessmen formally established the Hebrew Benevolent Society of Helena. Benevolent societies were common across the United States where there were substantial numbers of Jewish residents. Two Minute Books, preserved in the Montana Historical Society's Research Center archives, spanning 1866 to 1943, tell much about Helena's Jewish community and the challenges they overcame. Although Helena's Jews had no synagogue and no rabbi, as was often the case in the western communities, the Benevolent Society bound the group together. It maintained Jewish holidays, conducted prescribed rituals, offered financial assistance and medical care to the needy and encouraged charitable acts. A major purpose was to establish and maintain Hebrew burial grounds. The Minute Book details these early activities.

The Home of Peace, established in 1867 and tucked west of Capital High School, is Montana's oldest active Jewish cemetery and Helena's oldest cemetery. The first two burials recorded in the Minute Book, those of Emanuel Blum and H.L. Schlessinger, were re-interments from the mining camp cemetery on the grounds of present-day Central School. The two died before the founding of the Hebrew cemetery. The first twelve burials lie unmarked outside the cemetery's north boundary.

In 1869, the death of Mary Goldman demonstrated how the society grappled with questions of religious propriety without counsel of a rabbi. According to the *Helena Herald* on January 28 and February 4, 1869, Mary was not Jewish by birth but by adoption and choice. Described as "in her girlhood years," she apparently had not yet converted, or perhaps she was too young to do so. Controversy over her burial and the lack of a rabbi to resolve the question caused a lengthy delay in her burial. Society members ultimately granted her burial at the cemetery because of her innocence and her intent. Mary's spectacular funeral was the largest in Montana to that date. Four horses, draped and plumed in black, drew the hearse. Thirty single and double carriages and buggies, the teams of many of them also plumed in black, followed. Forty horsemen drew up the rear.

During this early period, the Home of Peace was Montana's only Jewish Cemetery and Jews from other communities were buried there. Although the first plat map of Virginia City shows a proposed Hebrew Burial Ground, the population was so fleeting that by the time the map was drawn in 1868, most residents had moved to Helena, and the cemetery there was never established. Solomon Content of Virginia City, who died in 1870, and B. Wolff of Deer Lodge, who died in 1872, are among the first twelve unmarked burials at the Home of Peace.

By 1867, Jews owned seventeen of Helena's twenty dry goods stores, and Jewish merchants and service providers had permanently settled with their families in the future capital. As Helena endured a series of devastating fires between 1869 and 1874, the Jewish community helped keep the fledgling mining camp solvent. Many Jewish merchants and businessmen had ties to a financial network that reached well beyond the Montana frontier, allowing access to financial resources to rebuild, sometimes again and again. Marcus Lissner lost his acclaimed, uninsured International Hotel in 1869, 1874 and 1879—so many times that it became known as the Phoenix. Each time he rebuilt. Like other Helena Jews, he financially helped others get started in business. Clothing merchant Jacob Feldberg lost his store several times. During one epic fire as his own store burned, firemen told the diminutive Feldberg to get out of their way because he was too little to help. Feldberg organized a bucket brigade and jumped rooftops to save his Fifth Avenue

A brick-paved walkway, reminiscent of a neighborhood, links family groups together at the Home of Peace Cemetery—Montana's oldest active Jewish cemetery. *From author.*

neighborhood from incineration. For his heroic act, citizens nicknamed him Helena's Paul Revere.

Membership in the Helena Board of Trade, forerunner of the chamber of commerce, was 20 percent Jewish in 1877. In 1881, Abram Sands was elected president of the organization. Marcus Lissner was elected to the city council six times, and Jewish citizens maintained some of Helena's most beautiful homes. The gentile community not only respected this socio-ethnic community but also embraced them. Jews were lawyers, judges, bankers, merchants, service providers and business partners with non-Jews.

The prestigious Montana Club, founded in 1885, counted prosperous, well-educated Jews, like clothier Herman Gans of the firm Gans and Klein, among its elite members. And Louis Kaufman partnered with gentile Louis Stadler to form one of Montana's largest cattle operations. Many of Helena's Jews, like other citizens, were also masons, and this affiliation drew Jews and gentiles together in fraternal brotherhood.

Helena's Jewish congregation remained organized without either a rabbi or a synagogue until 1889. Rabbi Samuel Schulman then came to lead Helena's congregation, bringing German Reform Judaism, which fit well with Helena's many Jews of German extraction. Under Rabbi Schulman, the congregation's dream of building the first "temple amidst the Rockies" reached fruition.

A committee formed to teach the gentile architects, Frederick Heinlein and Thomas F. Mathias, how to design the temple. Governor Joseph K. Toole, a Roman Catholic, laid the cornerstone in 1890, which was inscribed with the date 5651, according to the Jewish calendar. At the dedication in April 1891, congregation president Herman Gans accepted the key to the building, explaining to the crowd that the temple was meant to honor Helena's Jewish pioneers but also "to ornament the city" they loved. The stunning Moorish-style building was the first synagogue in the Pacific Northwest. Keyhole windows and twin towers crowned with exotic black-painted, star-spangled "onion" domes of Montana copper added significantly to Helena's cosmopolitan architecture.

As the second generation of Jewish pioneers came of age, the Helena congregation reached a peak in the 1890s. After 1900, educational opportunities and employment took many of this second generation out of the state. Into the twentieth century, the Minute Book records families moving away from Helena. In 1910, the Cemetery Association—the descendant of the Hebrew Benevolent Society—merged with the Congregation Emanu-El, confirming diminishing membership.

Helena continued to embrace the Jewish community. With the founding of the Helena YWCA in 1911, Frieda Fligelman was its first secretary. Frieda was so instrumental in its success that the Helena YWCA chose not to affiliate with the national organization. Its rule that non-Christians could

The stunning Moorish style Temple Emanu-El on Ewing Street added to Helena's cultural and architectural diversity. *From Parchen Drugs, Helena souvenir, 1891.*

not participate in management or decision making meant that Frieda, who was Jewish, could have no role. In 1972, Helena's YWCA was the nation's only independent chapter, and it did not affiliate until the 1980s.

As marriages between Jews and gentiles among Helena families became more frequent, cemetery rules relaxed. Before 1916, only people of the Jewish faith could be buried at the Home of Peace. Its board of trustees, however, realized that intermarriage was becoming prevalent and agreed to change this rule to include gentile spouses and their unmarried children and to allow non-Jewish funerals. That remains true today.

By the early 1930s, the small congregation could not maintain the temple. The State of Montana acquired the property for a token one dollar and a

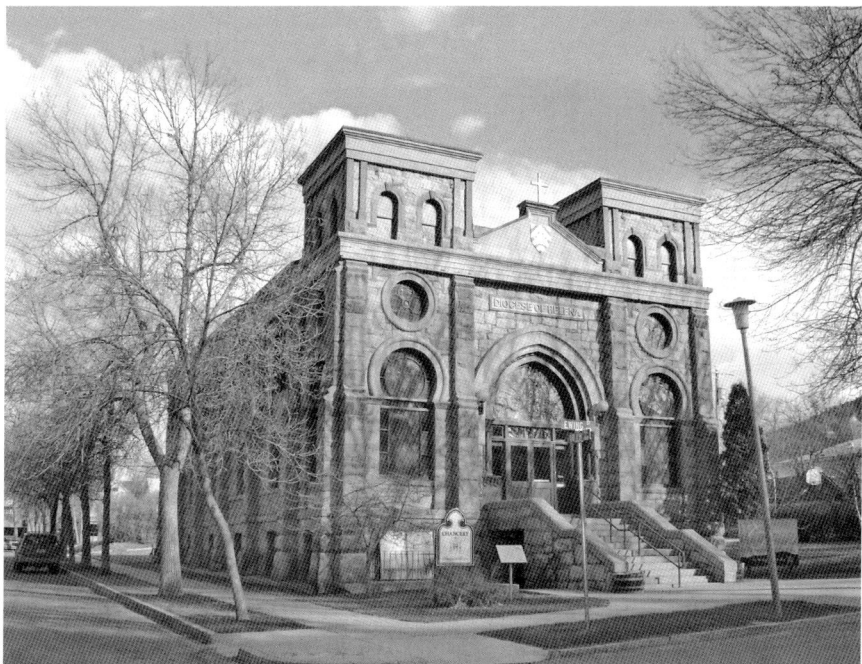

Divested of its copper domes and Hebrew inscriptions, the Temple Emanu-El now serves as the office for the Catholic Diocese of Helena. *From author.*

promise to use it for a "good and social purpose." Sandblasting the Hebrew inscription, "Gate to the Eternal," above the entry; removing the domes; and adding a second floor readied the building for state offices. The keyhole windows, stained glass and Hebrew year on the cornerstone were left undisturbed. At a time when preservation and adaptive reuse were hardly in an architect's vocabulary, the work reveals respectful planning. After housing State Social and Rehabilitation Services for decades, the Catholic Diocese of Helena purchased the property in 1981 for $83,000.

Both the Home of Peace and the former Temple Emanu-El, now diocesan offices, are listed in the National Register of Historic Places. The two Helena landmarks are a tribute to the pioneers who loved their adopted home. Jewish congregations today are growing in Helena and across Montana. Members may not be descendants of those pioneers, but they help perpetuate the legacy of those who came before them.

17

BUILDING A BETTER HELENA

The Southside Lime Kilns

By *Jon Axline*

About 350 million years ago, the Helena valley lay at the bottom of an inland sea. Billions of tiny marine creatures thrived in the water, and when they died their bodies settled into the muck on the seabed. After hundreds of millions of years of accumulation, and many more millions of years of geological heat and pressure, the muck metamorphosed into the pale gray rocks that are known today as Madison Limestone. The limestone is common throughout western and southwestern Montana. In Montana, the limestone beds range from one to two thousand feet thick in places. In Helena, the bed outcrops all along the south border of the valley at the base of the Boulder Batholith.

The presence of limestone in what would become Montana was first noted by the Lewis and Clark expedition in 1805. With the discovery of gold on Grasshopper Creek and Alder Gulch in the early 1860s, newspaper editors and promoters commented on the abundance of limestone in the territory. They were, however, far more concerned about limestone in proximity to mining operations for use in the smelting process than for use as a building material. Although lime burning occurred as an industry in Helena in the 1860s—and is represented by ruins in the south hills—it wasn't until 1875 that the first references to lime burning appeared in the territorial newspapers.

Early on, Helena's boosters recognized the benefits of the proximity of large outcrops of Madison Limestone. The Helena Board of Trade wrote in its 1887 report on the city's business conditions that "our renowned lime rock, which is found in the city limits…and towers above us from the crowning bluffs of Mount Helena in quantities that would furnish a hundred Londons, which burned into lime and mixed with our decomposed granite sand forms a cement that hardens as adamant when worked with brick and stone." Helena's fortunate proximity to extensive limestone outcrops was a recurring theme in promotional literature published about the Queen City in the late nineteenth century. In 1890, the board of trade wrote that "no city in the world is so abundantly supplied with building stone as Helena. Granite, sandstone, marble, porphyry, flag rock and lime rock are near our doors."

Since at least the seventeenth century, lime kilns assumed the basic design as those on Grizzly Gulch just south of Helena. Entrepreneurs built the kilns into hillsides to allow the easy transport and deposit of limestone into the open top of the kiln. Operators of early kilns placed the fuel for its firing at the base of the kiln and pulled the baked limestone out through holes in the front of the kilns. Locating and developing a lime kiln extended beyond the functional placement of the kiln near the limestone and fuel source. Placement was also based on the need to situate them away from populated areas "as they gave off noxious and potentially lethal gases." The development of the kilns reflected the logical placement far enough away from populated areas to avoid issues with potential off-gassing from the operation but close enough to serve potential customers in a practical and efficient manner. The lime kilns in hills south of Helena—like most kilns in the late nineteenth century in the United States—represented minimal capital investment, low cost of operation and good flexibility of operations.

Although great amounts of heat were required to produce the lime, making lime from limestone was relatively low tech. The kilns were situated next to and below the limestone quarries in locations where the stone proved easy to extract. Extraction consisted of quarrymen either prying loose the stone or blasting it away from the hillsides. They then conveyed the limestone by hand cars along a graded track or a ramp and dumped the material into the top of the kiln. From fire holes in the sides of the kiln, they heated the rock to 1,648° F and baked it for forty-eight hours. Fuel for the kilns was pine that was harvested in the surrounding hills. A kiln generally used three cords of wood every twenty-four hours and typically ran day and night for several days. At the end of that time, the workers allowed the fires to go out, cooling the limestone, which contracted and fell into the clean-out holes in the front of the kilns. The kiln's operators then pulled the limestone into the cooling

Joseph O'Neill's lime kilns did a booming business on Grizzly Gulch as Helena expanded in the 1880s. *From Pioneer Cabin Museum.*

shed from the clean-out hole. They stacked the material and pulverized the now-brittle limestone to a fine powder. Running day and night, a kiln could produce up to three tons of lime every day. Horse- or mule-drawn wagons then hauled the lime to the construction site, where it was slaked with water and mixed with sand for mortar and stucco.

One of the larger and noteworthy operations in the Helena area began in 1879 when Joseph O'Neill hired D.B.L. Cullough to construct a lime kiln on Grizzly Gulch for $2,500. A native of Massachusetts, O'Neill arrived in Helena in 1865 from Alder Gulch and operated a freighting business and livery stable on South Main Street. In 1867, he added lime burning to his many business ventures in the city. The kiln constructed by Cullough was the first built and operated under a patent he obtained for the process in 1875. O'Neill's kiln produced around 250 bushels of lime every twenty-four hours and burned about three cords of wood every day. In June 1884, the *Helena Independent* sent a reporter to the kiln. In the article, he described the lime burning process in Helena:

The kiln is built on a hillside, is about 30 feet high, is of solid granite walls and lined with fire brick. It is divided into three departments or stories. The lowest apartment is level with the bottom of the gulch and is enclosed within a large frame building, large enough to store many hundred bushels of lime. The opening of a large iron door in the kiln permits the dropping down, almost without assistance, of the lime which has been burned. In the second store, which is easily reached from the hillside, are three distinct furnaces—two which are in one side, and the third in the opposite side. The heat of these three furnaces is conducted in the center of the kiln, which chamber receives the lime rock at the top. The heat of the furnaces is very great; sufficient, it is thought, to melt readily ordinary ores.

By 1884, O'Neill operated two kilns on Grizzly Gulch with a third under construction. The building boom then sweeping Helena meant that the two completed kilns operated at full capacity. Unlike O'Neill's first kiln, the more recent kilns' structures included rubblestone cooling sheds in their construction. The limestone quarry that supplied the kilns was on the hillside above all three kilns. Prior to the construction of the iconic tower kilns, it is likely O'Neill operated pit kilns on the northwest side of Grizzly Gulch Road, opposite the later tower. While more expedient to construct, pit kilns were less efficient in their ability to produce lime compared to the tower-style kilns. The pit kilns had been "excavated in the soft earth at the sides of the gulch long ago and…were not designed to be of lasting character."

O'Neill operated the kilns until the onset of the Panic of 1893, when he leased them to James Kerwin and James McKelvey—a former O'Neill employee. In the late 1890s, the lease fell to McKelvey. The operation prospered until 1905, when competition from the Elliston Lime Company, twenty miles west of Helena, forced McKelvey to shutter his operation. While perhaps the best known, the O'Neill and Kerwin lime kilns weren't the only ones operating in the Helena vicinity. Kilns were also located on Lime Kiln and Oro Fino Gulches, near the Adams Street water reservoir east of Grizzly Gulch, and in the hills on the upper east side.

A lone lime kiln in a gulch on Helena's upper east side played a key role in Helena's development that is largely unknown today. Based on advertisements for lime manufacturers that appeared in Helena directories, lime operations expanded in the Helena area in the late 1880s. O'Neill and Kerwin's lime kilns on Grizzly Gulch appear in the directories from 1889 until 1901. William W. Winkleman operated a lime kiln near his residence on Hillsdale Avenue for a short time in the 1890s. He went on to do the

Today the Grizzly Gulch lime kilns still stand below the quarry that provided the raw materials for turning limestone into lime. *From Ellen Baumler Photograph.*

initial development work on the limestone quarry and kilns near Elliston. That operation now scars the hillside next to US Highway 12 near the intersection of Mullan Road. Other advertisements for lime manufacturers included one by two men, James Grant and John Marshall, who operated a lime kiln "east city limits south of Eighth Avenue."

James Grant arrived in Helena about 1888 and worked as a contractor, and Marshall was a carpenter. The two went into business together in 1889 and built the kiln. They used mine rails in the clean-out hole acquired from the adjacent Red Letter or Humboldt Lode mines or purchased from a Helena hardware store. Once the operation was up and running, Grant partnered with contractor Stephen Whalen in 1890. They won a contract to construct the second Helena High School, which stood prominently near the intersection of Lawrence Avenue and North Warren Street. The contractors completed construction of the granite three-story, Romanesque-style building in 1892. They needed enormous amounts of lime for the mortar and the interior plastering. The upper east side lime kiln provided the needed material. The men dissolved their business partnership upon completion of

The Grant-Marshall lime kiln on Helena's upper east side provided lime for the construction of the city's high school from 1890 to 1892. *From author.*

the high school, and both left Helena soon after. Whalen disappeared into history, but Grant went to work as a foreman and mason at the Montana Sandstone Company in Columbus, Montana. He likely quarried stone used to construct the Montana State Capitol from 1896 to 1902. Like Whalen, James Marshall is lost to history.

By World War I, the lime kilns around Helena were abandoned, victims of competition from the Elliston lime quarry and of changing construction methods. The Grizzly Gulch kilns are certainly an iconic and little-known part of Helena's landscape, though they played a critical role in Helena's vibrant history. Many of the historic buildings we venerate were built with lime derived from the limestone outcrops that once benefitted the city. The lime kilns now stand sentinel in the gulches south of the city and are, in some ways, like castle towers—a reminder of times long gone.

18

Haunting on Holter Street

By Ellen Baumler

On November 1, 1939, Del Lesson wrote in the *Helena Independent Record* that "every community should have some place that's haunted. There's a spine-tingling chill, an unearthly sensation about being in the presence of something 'haunted' that's good for our souls."

Helena has a few places that some consider haunted. Research proves that sometimes past events color the present and disturb the quiet we expect of our homes. The smell of cigar smoke, a waft of old perfume, footsteps in an empty room, a shadow in the night or marbles found in odd places might be evidence of unseen visitors. Most people have experienced events like these, but we don't usually linger on them.

One of these houses, where many occupants have come and gone for more than a century, is a lovely duplex. With a neat front yard and dramatic two-story bay windows, it sits along Holter Street in Helena's historic West Side neighborhood. Such high style, multi-family housing and prominent landlords and tenants illustrate the mobility of Helena's nineteenth-century population.

Reverend George K. Berry and his wife, Ida, arrived as newlyweds in 1888. Reverend Berry, pastor of the Christian Church at Power Street and Benton Avenue, partnered with Dr. Samuel Gilbert in real estate, each owning half the Holter Street lot. They built the two-story duplex—each identical side with seven generous rooms—circa 1889. Dr. Gilbert built the west half on speculation while the Berrys moved into the east half.

The *Independent* reported that Reverend Berry was among the "desirable" property-owning West Side neighborhood residents and predicted that the area would become Helena's Nob Hill.

The Berrys' occupancy was short lived when their boarder, Mrs. Rebecca Vail, hung herself in the back bedroom. Young Mrs. Vail had been married but a few days when her husband, Isaac, was murdered. She ended her life shortly after the Berrys took her in. The Berrys immediately moved out.

Dr. Calvin E. Nichols bought both sides of the duplex and in 1890 moved into the east half vacated by the Berrys. Dr. Nichols, a graduate of Bellevue Medical College in 1873, was a skilled physician. However, his membership in the Montana Medical Association was deferred because he stood accused of consulting with a homeopathic physician, a collaboration the medical profession did not approve. Dr. Nichols denied it but withdrew and returned to practice in New York. He continued to own the Holter Street duplex until 1907.

Theodore and Kate Shed briefly rented the east half of the duplex from Dr. Nichols in 1891. Theodore was well known as a key player in a violent Helena episode that had played out a few years previous. His father, Edward, owned the famous Kiyus Saloon, and father and son worked together off and on until Edward's death in 1877. Theodore eventually sold the business and worked as bookkeeper at the liquor and clothing business of Greenhood, Bohm and Company. He married Kate Lundwall, daughter of Swedish immigrants, in 1879. The couple had a son in 1881, named Edward Theodore after his grandfather and father.

On the evening of June 23, 1882, Theodore Shed was standing outside the Cosmopolitan Hotel when the Bozeman stage arrived. As passengers disembarked, John Hugle strode toward Shed and punched him hard. Shed instinctively fired his pistol and both men fell to the ground. The bullet passed through Hugle, nearly missing two men standing across the street. Hugle kept repeating, "Theo Shed shot me!" Shed was arrested.

The .38-caliber ball from an English bull dog–type pistol entered below Hugle's eye at such close range that there was gunpowder on Hugle's face and the smell of powder on his breath. Despite severe disfiguration, doctors hoped for recovery. Twenty-nine-year-old Hugle, however, died a few days later.

Shed and Hugle, co-workers at Greenhood and Bohm, had a long-standing feud over a buffalo coat of Shed's. Employees frequently borrowed the coat, but when Hugle put it on, Shed objected, insisting that he could use it but only with permission. Hugle declined, and afterward, the men never spoke to each other. The immediate difficulty between the two was unknown. Friends described both as high-strung. Shed was of small stature, while Hugle was tall and muscular. Although Hugle was unarmed, he was capable of seriously injuring the smaller man.

Suffering mental torture, extreme remorse and serious health issues, Shed finally left the crowded county jail a month later on $6,000 bond. His murder trial in November 1883 resulted in acquittal of second-degree murder. Perhaps because of his own legal trouble, Shed relocated to Marysville, where he opened a law practice and served as justice of the peace. Then in 1889, eight-year-old Eddie died of unknown causes. The loss of their only child devastated the Sheds. The grief-stricken couple moved to Helena and briefly rented the east half of the duplex. They did not stay long on Holter Street, but when they moved out, perhaps they did not leave the house empty.

For current owners Steve Faherty and Anthony "Tony" Wilson, the duplex the Sheds occupied has yielded some eerie experiences and coincidences. Their extensive research has revealed a few deaths, many families with children and the spectacular suicide of Rebecca Vail. Some, but not all, of their experiences seem to align with the Sheds and the energy they may have initiated.

There were tenants on both sides when Steve and Tony bought the duplex in 2010. Parents of the east half tenants came to help them pack, but they still had a month on their lease and did not intend an immediate move. When Tony noticed a U-Haul out front and went to check, the mother rushed out, crying hysterically that they were hearing footsteps on the basement stairs at night. Not only did they move out that day, but the single mom in the west half also moved out at the same time. She claimed that her children were talking and playing with children who were not there. Coincidentally, it was Halloween.

Tony and Steve moved into the east half. They had lived there for several years, and during that time, they occasionally heard noises like footsteps coming up the basement stairs. They had heard similar stories from other tenants, but they figured it was just furnace noises.

It was Halloween again when a rattling noise in the pocket doors between the living and dining rooms distracted Tony. He clearly saw a little boy dressed in dark clothing and a wide-brimmed hat. He was bent down close to the floor, chasing something that was not there. He ran through the living and dining rooms and disappeared.

Sometime later, a portrait of Eddie Shed came to light. He wore dark clothing and, like his dad, was of small stature. Eddie had died on

November 4, 1889. It occurred to Tony that odd events occurred around the end of October and early November. Maybe the single mom's children really did have a ghostly playmate. Maybe Eddie was somehow stuck in time, looking for his parents.

A former owner had returned the original light fixtures from the duplex's west half. There were seven—one for each room—of heavy wrought iron suspended on chains. Steve spent a morning installing them. He came back from lunch to find every fixture on the floor, though they had not fallen. The newly refinished floors were unmarked—the glass shades unbroken. Steve also began to find 1880–1900s vintage marbles, dozens of them, wherever he had been working. Once, when he dug a trench to install a pipe in the basement, he left it open. When he came back, there was a neat line of marbles in the trench.

During the summer of 2018, as painters prepared to work on the house, the contractor took photos. One shot revealed the silhouette of an older

Dozens of antique marbles collected from the Holter Street duplex add to its mystique. *From Tony Wilson.*

Bullet casings and a nineteenth-century button hook for men's spats are among the artifacts homeowners recovered from the Holter Street residence. *From Tony Wilson.*

woman in the front bedroom window of the east half. Soon after, one of the painters lost his balance and fell from the top story, sustaining permanent injuries. He claimed that someone screamed at him, and he lost his balance. There was no one around.

The project dragged on into October. Late in the month, the painters called Steve in a panic. They had been using a power sander on the east half. All three painters claimed that a very angry older man had appeared in the dining room window, cursing and yelling at them to stop the noise.

There was no one in the house at the time except Branson the dog, who seemed undisturbed.

Most recently, Steve cleaned the basement, got rid of all the trash and swept the floor. When he later returned, he found a can of shoe polish, a vintage beer can and a train ticket from San Francisco to Helena on the floor. The ticket bore the name of Jim Gleason, a past resident, who died in 1943. It was dated October 31, 1937.

For Steve and Tony, despite the surprising and sometimes unsettling events, the house is full of good energy. They are responsible stewards of the historic property and have made every effort to understand its history and the people who came before them. And when Halloween draws near, they have learned to expect the unexpected.

19

THE GREAT CANYON FERRY FLYING SAUCER HOAX

By Jon Axline

Montanans saw a lot of strange things that defied explanation during the 1960s, not the least of which were unexplained objects in the skies, or in the case of Canyon Ferry, on the ground. In April 1964, a flying saucer allegedly landed on the outskirts of Canyon Ferry Village and garnered national headlines. But was it the real thing or just a hoax perpetrated by a group of youngsters?

Late in the evening of April 29, 1964, eleven-year-old Linda Davis saw a strange glow reflecting on the curtains of her bedroom in her house on the cul-de-sac of Bonner Park Road. She was the daughter of Bert and Louise Davis; Bert was the superintendent of the Bureau of Reclamation's Canyon Ferry Project. Linda jumped off her bed and ran outside, where her fifteen-year-old brother, Thom, was goofing around with a group of neighborhood kids. Thom and Linda ran to the fence and saw something they couldn't explain: a pulsing, white, egg-shaped object about the size of an automobile standing on four legs in a barren field about two hundred feet behind their house. They called over their three friends, while neighbor Bill Behenny phoned the Lewis and Clark County sheriff's office. As the kids approached the object, it took off with a whoosh and disappeared over Canyon Ferry Lake to the south. The entire incident lasted just a few minutes start to finish, but the investigation lasted much longer and took a heavy toll on the young witnesses and their parents.

While the Davis kids and their friends were building up their courage to approach the object, long-time county sheriff Dave Middlemas told Behenny to have an adult investigate the sighting. He believed it to be a prank, especially since the annual Vigilante Day Parade was just a few days away. Middlemas was surprised when Bert Davis called him back an hour later. With that call, the sheriff dispatched two deputies to investigate. They found five youngsters still shaken by what they saw, along with physical evidence that something had indeed happened on the outskirts of town. At the alleged landing site, two deputies found four holes in the earth about thirteen feet apart in a square pattern. The holes were cone shaped and about six to eight inches in diameter. Offset in the center of the square was a scorched patch about four feet in diameter. Something had been there, but whether it was a hoax or from an alien spacecraft was not known.

This was enough for the sheriff to notify the Malmstrom Air Force Base in Great Falls. The following day, five air force investigators arrived in Canyon Ferry Village and questioned each of the witnesses at length. They also spent a considerable amount of time at the landing site, taking measurements and soil samples. The questioning was intense enough that Thom Davis finally admitted that he didn't know what he saw, if anything at all. At the end of the day, air force spokesman Colonel H.L. Newfield, who was dubious of the sighting, told the press, "We are not at liberty to say anything at this point, I'm not sure we will make a positive statement about this anytime."

Meanwhile, the village had become a mecca for curiosity seekers. So much so that parking places were at a premium, and the children who saw the object were badgered by reporters for statements. One local resident, a UFO enthusiast with a large book collection on the subject, conducted her own investigation. Pointing to an illustration in one of her books, she asked, "Did it look like this?" When answered in the affirmative, she stated, "Well, you probably saw a flying saucer."

Even the Cheerio Lounge in Helena's Placer Hotel got into the act. In an advertisement in the *Independent Record*, it boasted, "You'll go 'Who-o-o-osh' like the Canyon Ferry saucer after one of our jumbo martinis!"

Evidence for and against the incident is suggestive. In its favor was the obvious impact the event had on the witnesses. Although the air force's rigorous questioning left one of the witnesses in doubt, the remaining four were sure they saw something. Their parents defended them as well. Some residents of the village reported that their televisions blacked out or had snowy reception at the time the incident took place. Some fishermen reported seeing a bright white light over the reservoir prior to the landing.

Five days before the Canyon Ferry incident, a New Mexico patrolman observed an object land in a gulch near Socorro. The case remains unexplained. *From ufo-explorer.com.*

But evidence also pointed to a hoax. The smell left behind by the object had the distinct odor of kerosene or diesel. Fresh dirt was scattered over the alleged landing site. Importantly, five days before the Canyon Ferry sighting, a patrolman from Socorro, New Mexico, Lonnie Zamora, encountered an egg-shaped object standing on four legs outside the city in an isolated arroyo. The incident attracted nationwide attention and is still officially listed as unknown. Each of the Canyon Ferry kids had heard about the Socorro incident.

Flying Saucer sightings in the Helena area was nothing new. The first recorded sighting, in July 1948, may have been floating milkwood seeds misinterpreted as flying discs. In July and August 1950, Helena experienced a real flap. There were at least three reported UFO sightings in the space of just thirty days. The most suggestive took place on July 18, when several Helenans reported a flaming flying disc buzzing in the Helena area. On August 13, Mrs. Estella Welch reported seeing a flying saucer that resembled two soup plates put together as she walked home from a Rodney Street grocery. When a newspaper reporter asked about what she saw, Mrs. Welch stated, "Truman, nor nobody else, can tell they don't exist—I saw this one!"

So, what did Thom and Linda Davis and their friends see, if anything, in April 1964? While reports circulated that the air force had concluded it was "a hoax perpetrated by children who wanted to play a trick on a younger sister," the air force denied the claim and never made an official determination about the sighting. Linda Davis's mother, and others in Canyon Ferry Village, believed their kids had seen something and criticized the air force's handling of the investigation. But Thom Davis admitted to investigator Joan Bird that the whole thing was a hoax. A damn good hoax, as it convinced many investigators and UFO enthusiasts that Canyon Ferry was the scene of a close encounter with the unknown.

20

BRYANT SCHOOL'S
UNUSUAL FRIENDS

By Ellen Baumler

Historic Bryant School in Helena's Sixth Ward nurtured thousands of students. Like so many other elementary schools across Montana, its atmosphere was charged with loud and enthusiastic children whose voices echoed through the hallways. Bryant's current student experience, however, is not like that of students elsewhere. There is still a special energy that most staff and students readily acknowledge that adds dimension to the usual school experiences. This was especially true of the several years from 2017 to 2019, leading up to the move to a new Bryant School next door.

When the first Northern Pacific engine arrived in Helena on newly laid tracks at the makeshift Sixth Ward depot in 1883, it assured Helena's permanence. The historic commercial area around the depot—listed in the National Register of Historic Places—quickly boomed to serve workers, shopkeepers and passengers. The district today includes Helena's only remaining brick-paved street with embedded trolley tracks, the last row of 1880s false front buildings and the 1905 depot designed by renowned architect Charles A. Reed. (Reed's architectural firm supervised the construction of New York City's famed Grand Central Station.) These survivors recall the traffic that once bustled between the depot and its boardinghouses, hotels and shops. Bryant School features prominently in the residential neighborhood fringing the commercial district.

Families settling in the new Sixth Ward demanded city services, and by 1884, a depot school was being planned. The Northern Pacific donated three lots, and the school board purchased a fourth at Boulder Avenue and Harris Street. By mid-October 1885, the two-room school, officially named the Sixth Ward School, was in use and nearly complete. Two more rooms were added in 1888, and by 1890, there were 112 students in the first and second grades. An additional wing again increased capacity to six rooms. By this time, the school had again been renamed after American poet, journalist and editor William Cullen Bryant.

The first Bryant School was razed and rebuilt on the same site in 1913. When earthquakes rocked the Helena valley in October 1935, damage in the Sixth Ward was extensive. Bryant School was a near-total loss. Bryant students, grades one through eight, attended makeshift classes in basement rooms at Central School until December 1937, when the new Bryant was finally finished. The new Art Deco–style school, the third school on the original site, featured one story with eight classrooms on the first floor. The basement of the old school was reused and reconfigured. It included boys' and girls' shower rooms, a nurse's room, a large playroom and the boiler

The first Bryant School, enlarged from its original two rooms to six rooms, was replaced in 1913. *From Parchen Drugs, Helena souvenir, 1891.*

Built after the 1935 earthquakes, the third Bryant School served the Sixth Ward until its replacement in 2019. *From author.*

salvaged from the old building. The basement later served as the school cafeteria, and more recently, it housed special education and music classes.

When the school district committed to building a new Bryant in 2017, students and staff began noticing subtle changes. Everyone was excited, but it was more than that. The energy in the old building seemed to ramp up as the big move—projected for fall 2019—drew nearer. Bryant staff and students, always keenly aware of their school's longevity, began to experience events that suggested the school's past was in many ways entangled in the present.

Knocking in the basement crawlspaces, the distinct smell of cigar smoke, music drifting out of the locked music room and footsteps in empty hallways became commonplace for many who spent time in the old building. Literacy coach Justine Alberts was new to Bryant and unaware of these spirited quirks. It scared her when teacher Jesika Fisher announced at a staff meeting that "the ghost" had called her. Jesika explained that she had been working late. The custodian was the only other person in the building. Classroom phones connect with other classrooms, and when Jesika's phone rang, she could see that the call was coming from Bridget Butler, though Bridget was not there. Jesika answered the phone, knowing that there would be no one on the line.

This event frightened Justine, and she confessed her fear to librarian Joice Franzen. They were in the library as Joice tried to reassure her, finally remarking, "Well, maybe something just needs to happen to dispel your fears." At that moment, a book fell off a shelf and hit the floor. Joice nonchalantly picked it up and put it back without comment. Later, Justine tried everything she could think of to make the book fall off that shelf. It could not be done. After that, like everyone else at Bryant, Justine was not afraid but rather now views such unexplained experiences as interesting.

Joice and others reportedly saw a young boy in various rooms, and some people may have experienced his mischief. One teacher was in the basement teacher's room cutting various colors of Valentine hearts. When she added a pink one to the stack, it inexplicably slid off to one side. The next pink one slid off in the opposite direction. None of the others moved. When a third pink heart lifted and came toward her, she cut no more pink hearts that day. Returning later to finish, she cut many pink hearts, and they all stayed put. Another teacher liked to bounce a soccer ball against his classroom wall. The boys' restroom was on the other side. One student told the teacher, "The boy in the bathroom doesn't like you bouncing the ball."

Once, speech pathologist Andrea Martin Salazar was alone in her basement classroom. She got up to close her door and returned to her seat. The doorknob rattled loudly, like someone was trying to get in. There was no one nearby. Another time, Andrea heard footsteps and assumed a student had come in and walked behind a partition. She waited a few minutes, and when no one came out, she went to get the student, but no one was there.

So many students and staff have come and gone at Bryant that it is impossible to say if these events were tied to one person, or who this boy was. But there is one theory. In February 1935, before the October earthquakes, a popular Bryant fourth grader was hit by a car on a poorly lit street and died instantly. Perhaps he returned to run down the hallways, make music and play tricks.

Joice not only encountered the youngster but also saw a man in a hat. She watched him stride across the floor and walk through a bookcase. Later, teachers sorting through old photographs found a picture of John G. Black, Bryant's longtime custodian. Joice easily identified him as the man she saw. Mr. Black served Bryant from 1929 to 1962, through the tragic death of the fourth grader, the earthquakes, the rebuilding of Bryant in

Bryant School's students and staff placed a plaque at the base of the flagpole honoring their beloved custodian, Mr. John G. Black. *From author.*

1937, his marriage to Hilda Pifer in 1941 and Hilda's death in 1952. The much-loved custodian, sporting a hat and cigar, always arrived early to ring the bell. Bryant commemorated his service with a plaque at the base of the flagpole.

Mr. Black championed students and watched over them. Not long ago, as students came in from recess, a student in Lonnie Brooks's class said to her, "Mr. Black let the mean ones in." Students later claimed that there was a man sitting in one of their chairs. They said that although they could not see him, the chair was too heavy to move. Lonnie declined to test it. And as teacher Erin Finstad worked after hours on her master's degree, she got quite used to the smell of Mr. Black's cigar smoke.

Like Justine Alberts, Title I teacher Kristie Baerlocher was new to Bryant and completely unaware of her colleagues' experiences. She and a student were alone in the basement music room, working at the computer. The girl began squinting and shaking her head. Thinking she probably needed a break, Kristie asked what was wrong. The girl matter-of-factly replied, "All these faces staring at me are irritating." The student then began staring at a corner of the room. Kristie finally asked what was in the corner. Again, the girl answered matter-of-factly, "There's a lady there in a pretty white dress." A few minutes later, the student's head moved as she seemed to follow something across the room. "She's gone," said the student, and the incident was over.

Night custodian Harlan Schmitt probably experienced more than anyone. He saw the little red-headed boy, had footsteps follow him and experienced his equipment turn on by itself. From the basement, he heard someone running past the office overhead. Harlan took it in stride but sometimes used strong words when it interfered with his work. He was frightened only once. As he swept the hall floor in front of the office, something came at him from behind, and his arms and legs turned to mush. He sat down feeling very strange. Five minutes later, he felt the energy rush out, and he was fine.

Everyone wondered if these experiences would continue after the move. Harlan says that as the new school was under construction, he sometimes saw a shadowy figure moving in the windows of the new school. Was it a reflection—a trick of the eye?

No traces remain of the old Bryant School. Students moved into the new Bryant in the fall of 2019. Time will tell if Mr. Black accompanied them.

Bibliography

American Memory Map Collection. Library of Congress, Washington, D.C. https://loc.gov.

Axline, Jon. "Operation Skywatch: The Montana Ground Observer Corps, 1952–1959." *Montana: The Magazine of Western History* 67, no. 2 (Summer 2017).

———, et al. *More from the Quarries of Last Chance Gulch*. 3 vols. Helena, MT: The Independent Record, 1995–1998.

Baumler, Ellen. "Forgotten Pioneers: The Chinese in Montana." *Montana: The Magazine of Western History* 65, no. 2 (Summer, 2015).

———. *Helena: The Town That Gold Built*. San Antonio, TX: HPNbooks, 2014.

———. *Montana Moments*. Helena, MT: MHS Press, 2010.

———. *More Montana Moments*. Helena, MT: MHS Press, 2012.

———. "We Are Learning to Do These Things Better: A Women's History of Helena's First Neighborhood." *Montana: The Magazine of Western History* 64, no. 3 (Autumn, 2014).

Bird, Joan. *Montana UFOs*. Helena, MT: Riverbend, 2012.

Campbell, William C. *From the Quarries of Last Chance Gulch Volume I*. Helena, MT: Montana Record, 1951.

———. *From the Quarries of Last Chance Gulch Volume II*. Helena, MT: Independent Record, 1964.

Donovan, Roberta, and Keith Wolverton. *Mystery Stalks the Prairie*. Raynesford, MT: T.H.A.R. Institute, 1976.

Donovan, Tom. *Hanging Around the Big Sky: The Unofficial Guide to Lynching, Strangling, and Legal Hangings of Montana Book 1.* Great Falls, MT: Portage Meadows, 2007.

General Land Office Records. "The Official Federal Land Records Site." U.S. Department of the Interior. https://glorecords.blm.gov.

Hanchett, Leland J. *Montana's Benton Road.* Wolf Creek, MT: Pine Rim, 2008.

Helena City Directories. Omaha, NE: R.L. Polk and Company, 1883.

Home of Peace Cemetery Associations Records, 1865–1943. Home of Peace Cemetery Association Montana Historical Society Research Center Archives. MC 38. Helena, MT.

Malone, Michael P., Richard Roeder, and William L. Lang. *Montana: A History of Two Centuries.* Rev. ed. Seattle: University of Washington Press, 1991.

Merritt, Christopher W. *The Coming Man from Canton: Chinese Experience in Montana, 1862–1943.* Lincoln: University of Nebraska Press, 2017.

Montana Historical Society Vertical Files. Montana Historical Society Research Center. Helena. Montana.

National Register of Historic Places Nomination Forms. State Historic Preservation Office. Helena, MT.

Paladin, Vivian A. *Valleys of the Prickly Pear.* Helena, MT: Little Red Schoolhouse, 1988.

———, and Jean Baucus. *Helena: An Illustrated History.* Helena: Montana Historical Society Press, 1996.

Phillips, Paul C. *Medicine in the Making in Montana.* Bozeman: Montana State University Press, 1962.

Sanborn-Perris Fire Insurance Maps of Helena. Pelham, NY: Sanborn Map Company, 1884–1951.

Sanders, W.F., II, and Robert Taylor. *Biscuits and Badmen: The Sanders Story in Their Own Words.* Butte, MT: Editorial Review Press, 1983.

Spalding, Charleen. *Benton Avenue Cemetery: A Pioneer Resting Place.* Helena, MT: Pioneer Tales, 2010.

United States Census Records. www.ancestry.com.

Newspapers

Anaconda Standard
Butte Miner
Great Falls Tribune

Helena Independent
Helena Independent Record
Helena Weekly Herald
Montana Post (Virginia City)
Montana Standard (Butte)
New North-West (Deer Lodge)
River Press (Fort Benton)

INDEX

B

Baucus, John 25
Bear's Tooth (Teeth) 20
Benton Avenue Cemetery 49
Benton Road 13, 14, 15, 16, 18,
    24, 39, 40, 41, 43
Black, John G. 116
Brewer, Henrietta 76, 78, 80
Bridge Street 18, 26, 27, 28, 29, 30,
    50, 52
Bryant School 113, 114
Bullock, Seth 35, 38
Bureau of Air Commerce 65, 66,
    68, 69

C

Calvary Cemetery 59, 60
Canyon Ferry Village 110
Cheerio Lounge 111
Chinatown 81, 83, 84, 86
Chinese 41, 81, 82, 83, 84, 85, 86

Clarke, Coth-co-co-na 21, 22
Clarke, Malcolm 20
Clark, William 13
Clayton, Leroy 87
Clayton, Mattie 90, 91
Confederate Gulch 13
Connor, Linnie 56, 57, 58
Cruse, Mamie 59
Curran, W.J. 41, 42

D

Deadwood, South Dakota 35, 38
Dean, Dr. Maria 76, 77, 78, 79, 80
Decker, Aileen 73, 75
Deer Lodge 13, 30, 32, 33, 93

E

Emerson, Blanche 52, 53

F

false front buildings 27
Fergus, James 22, 23, 24
Fergus, Pamelia 22
Fligelman, Frieda 95
Forestvale Cemetery 79, 83
Fort Benton 13, 14, 20, 30, 37, 41
Fort MacKenzie 44
Four Georgians 9, 26
Frenchwoman's Road 31

G

Glass, Andrew 14, 41, 42, 43
Glass, Johannah 42, 43
Grandstreet Theatre 48
Grimes, Tom 24
Guyot, Constant 31, 33
Guyot, Madame 32, 33, 34

H

hanging tree 26
Helena Board of Trade 94
Helena Public Library 46
House of the Good Shepherd 55, 56, 59
Hugle, John 105, 106

I

Indian trails 14

J

Jewish pioneers 92, 95
Juisto, Chere 9

K

Kohrs, Conrad 28
Kurtz, Leanne 9

L

Lea, Bob 61, 62, 63, 64
Lewis and Clark County 10, 25, 35, 36, 48, 110
Lewis and Clark County Jail 37
Lewis and Clark Library 44, 45, 48, 83

M

MacDonald Pass 31, 66, 68, 69
Marshall, Doris 86
Meloy, Harriett 10
Merrill, Agnes 52, 54
Middlemas, Dave 111
Mitchell, Martin 24
Montana City 20
Montana Post 33, 34, 44, 45
Morrison, Kim 10
Mullan, John 13, 20
Mullan Road 14, 30

N

National Parks Airway 68
Northern Pacific Railroad 76
Northern Transcontinental Airway 65, 68

O

Old North Trail 20
Operation Skywatch 71

P

Paladin, Vivian 10, 11
Prickly Pear Valley 20, 21, 24

R

Roeder, Richard 9, 10

S

Sanders, Harriett 45
Sanders, Wilbur Fisk 44, 45
Sandoval, Good Singing 21
Sears, Caleb 40
Seven Mile House 39, 40, 41, 42, 43
Shaffer, Frederick 36, 37
Shed, Edward "Eddie" 106
Shed, Theodore 105, 106
Shors, Dave 9
Sieben, Henry 24
Sieben Ranch 20, 25
Silver City 15, 18, 40, 41, 43
Sing, Lee 41, 42
Sixth Ward 76, 113, 114
Sleeping Giant 23, 68
Spencer, Fannie 52, 54
Sterres, William 36, 37, 38
St. Peter's Hospital 76

T

Temple Emanu-El 92, 97

U

Unitarian Church 48

V

Virginia City, Montana 13, 28, 44, 45, 52, 93

W

Walter, Dave 9, 10
Warl, Franz 36, 37, 38
Wheatley, William 36, 37, 38
Wheeler, Mary 80
Whitford, C.S. 34
Whitlatch, James 44
Whittenberg, Bruce 10
Wolverton, Keith 63, 64
Wood Street 30, 52

Y

Young, Georgia C. 77, 78, 79, 80
YWCA 79, 95

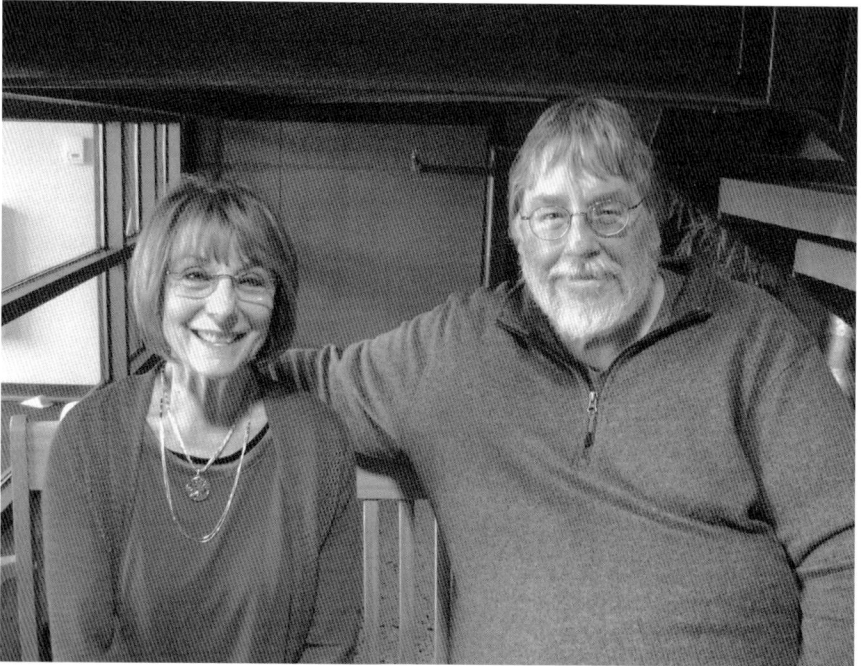

About the Authors

Ellen Baumler received her PhD in English, history and classics from the University of Kansas, where she was a fourth-generation Jayhawk. She was the interpretive historian at the Montana Historical Society in Helena, Montana from 1992 until her retirement in 2018. She has been a teacher and is an extraordinary tour guide, and she is passionate about sharing Montana's lesser-known history. A longtime member of the Humanities Montana Speakers Bureau, Baumler's expert storytelling has delighted audiences of all ages and interests across the state. She is a 2011 recipient of the Governor's Award for Humanities and an award-winning author of many books and articles on diverse topics. She is best known for her spine-tingling, well-researched stories on Montana's haunted places.

Jon Axline is the long-time historian at the Montana Department of Transportation (MDT). When not sweating over the state's historic roads and bridges, he conducts cultural resource surveys and writes the MDT's roadside historical and geological interpretive markers. Jon was a regular contributor to *Montana Magazine* and *Montana: The Magazine of Western History*. He is the author of *Conveniences Sorely Needed: Montana's Historic Highway Bridges*, as well as the editor of *Montana's Historical Highway Markers*, *Taming Big Sky Country: A History of Montana Transportation from Trails to Interstates* and *The Beartooth Highway: A History of America's Most Beautiful Drive*. Jon lives in Helena with his wife and four dogs.

Visit us at
www.historypress.com